This Coloring Book Belongs To

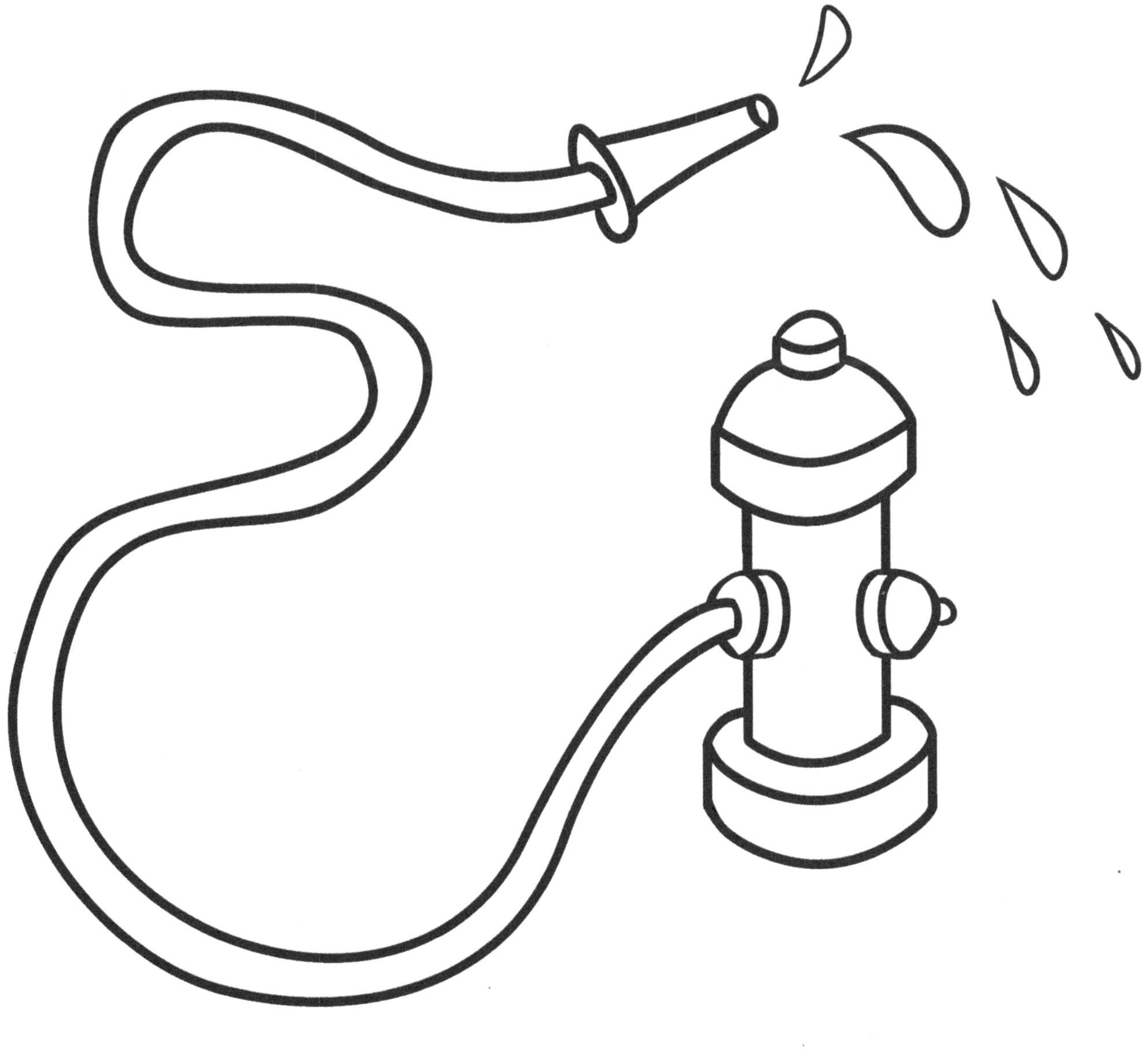

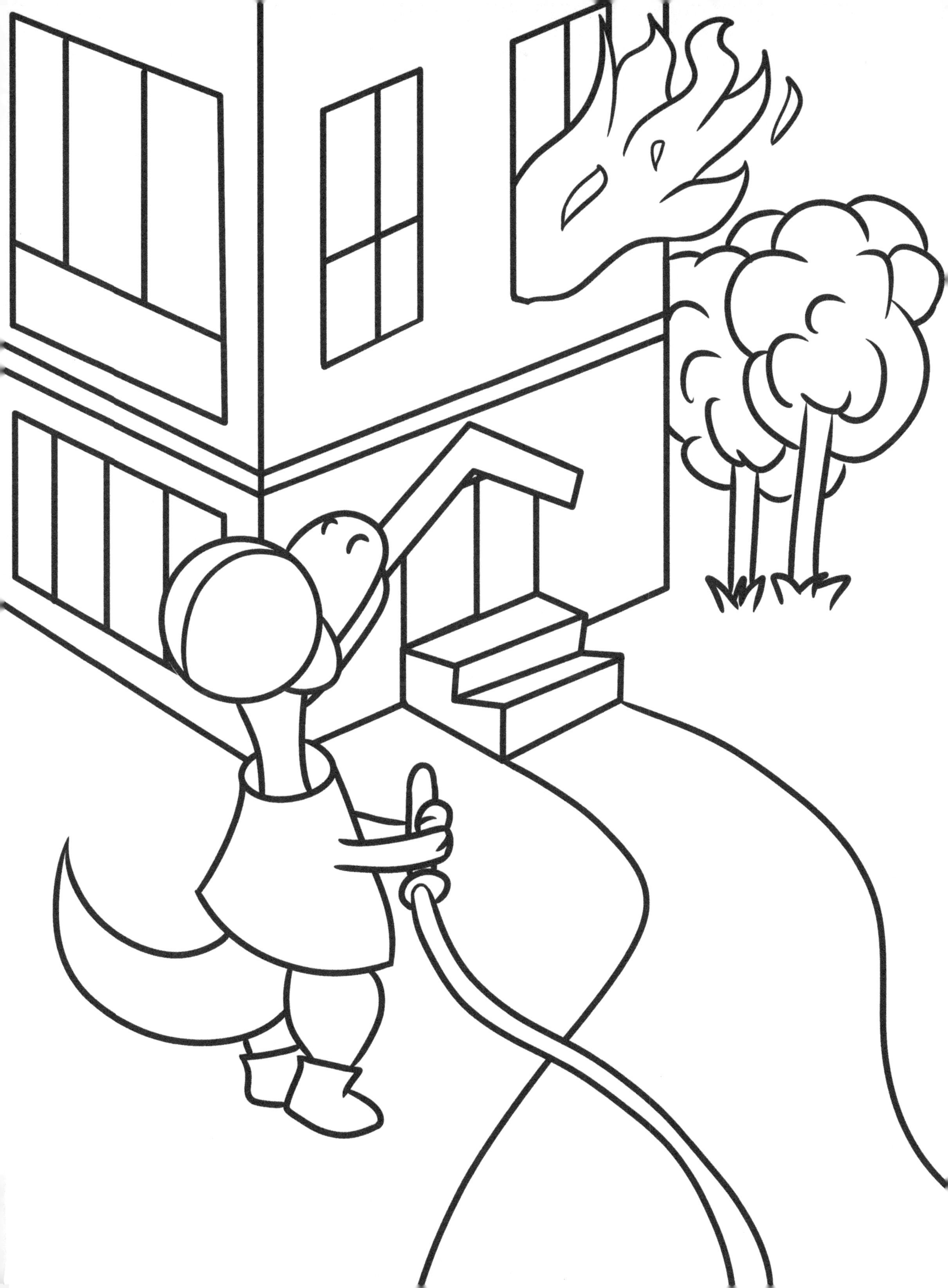

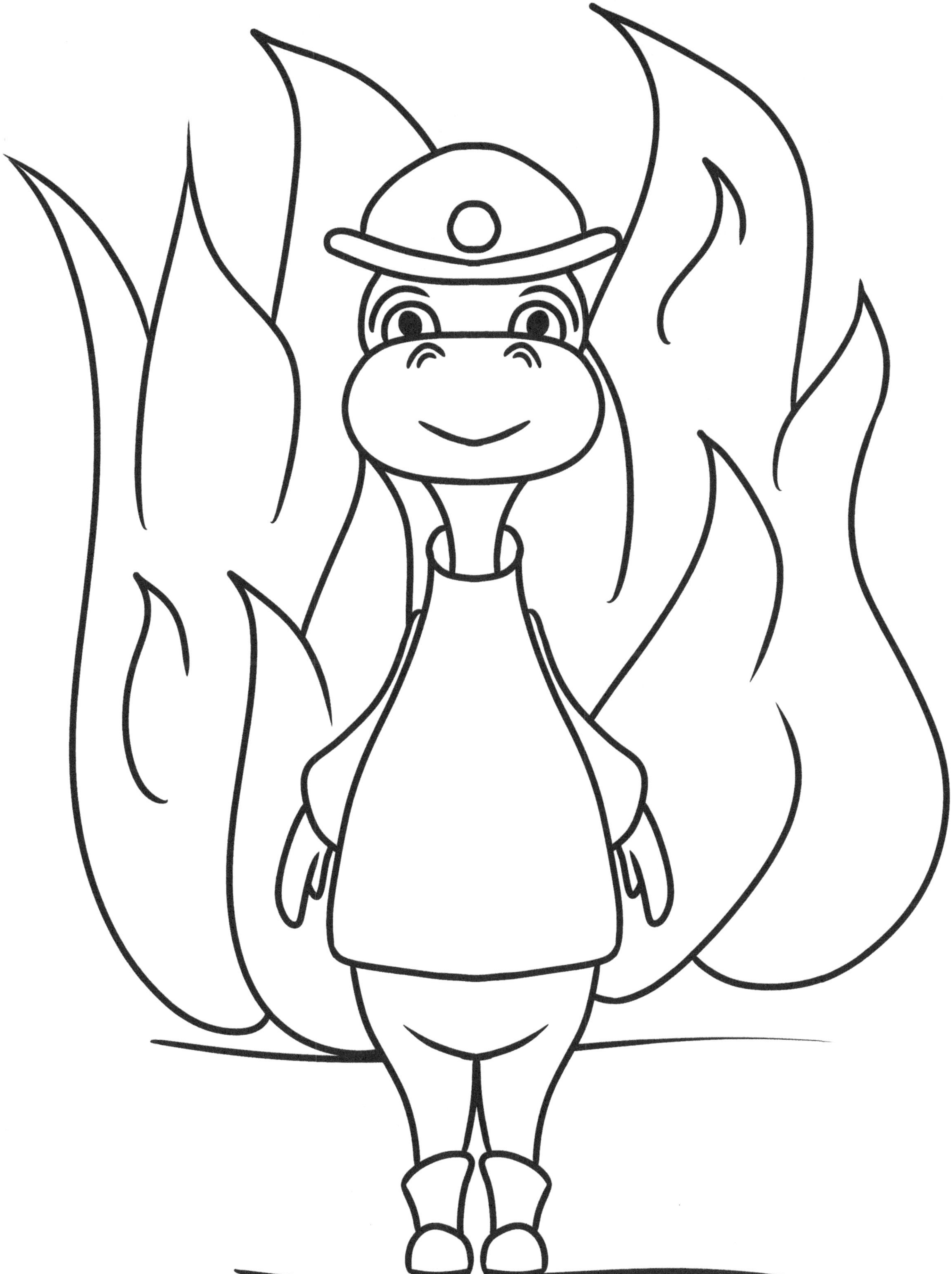

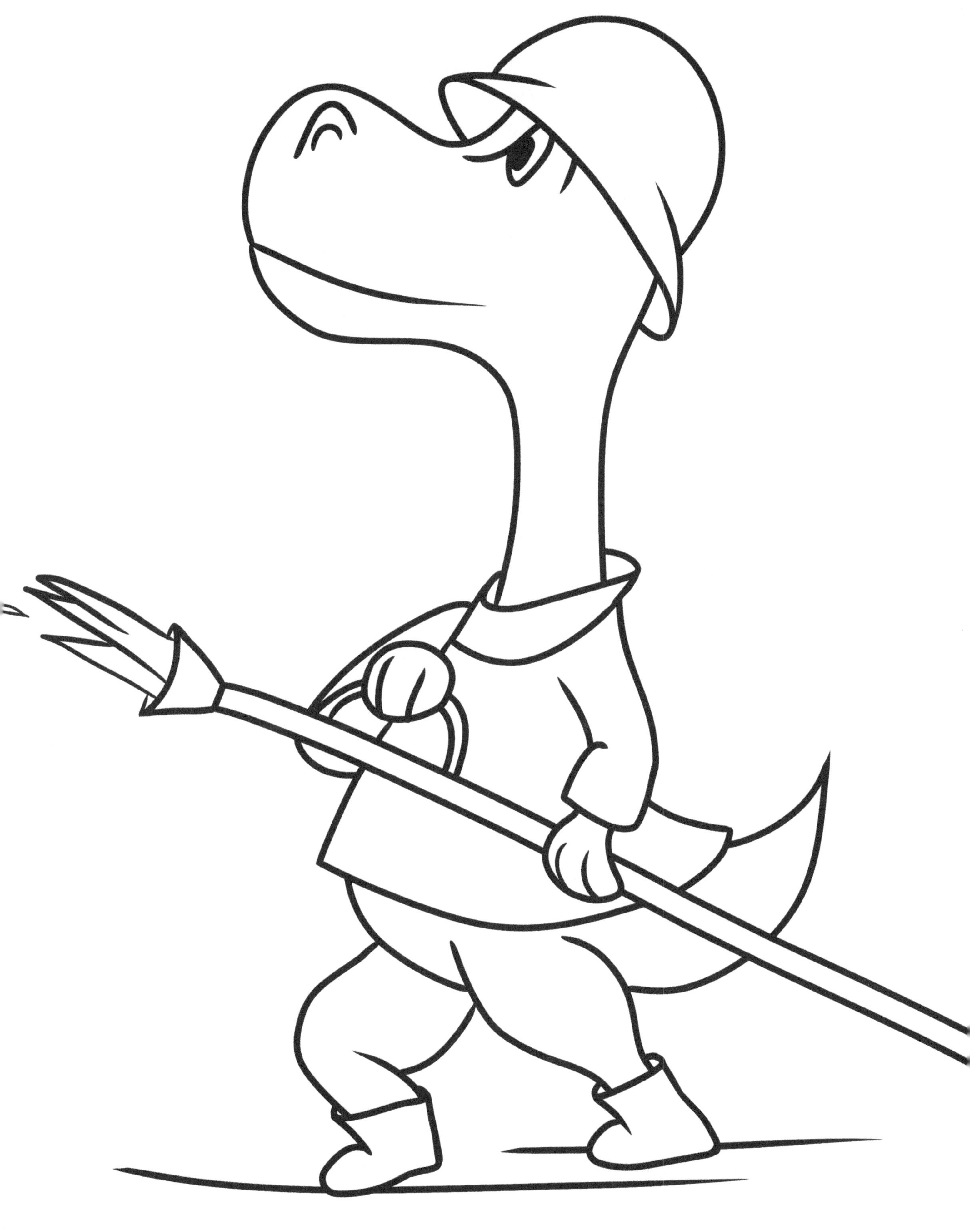

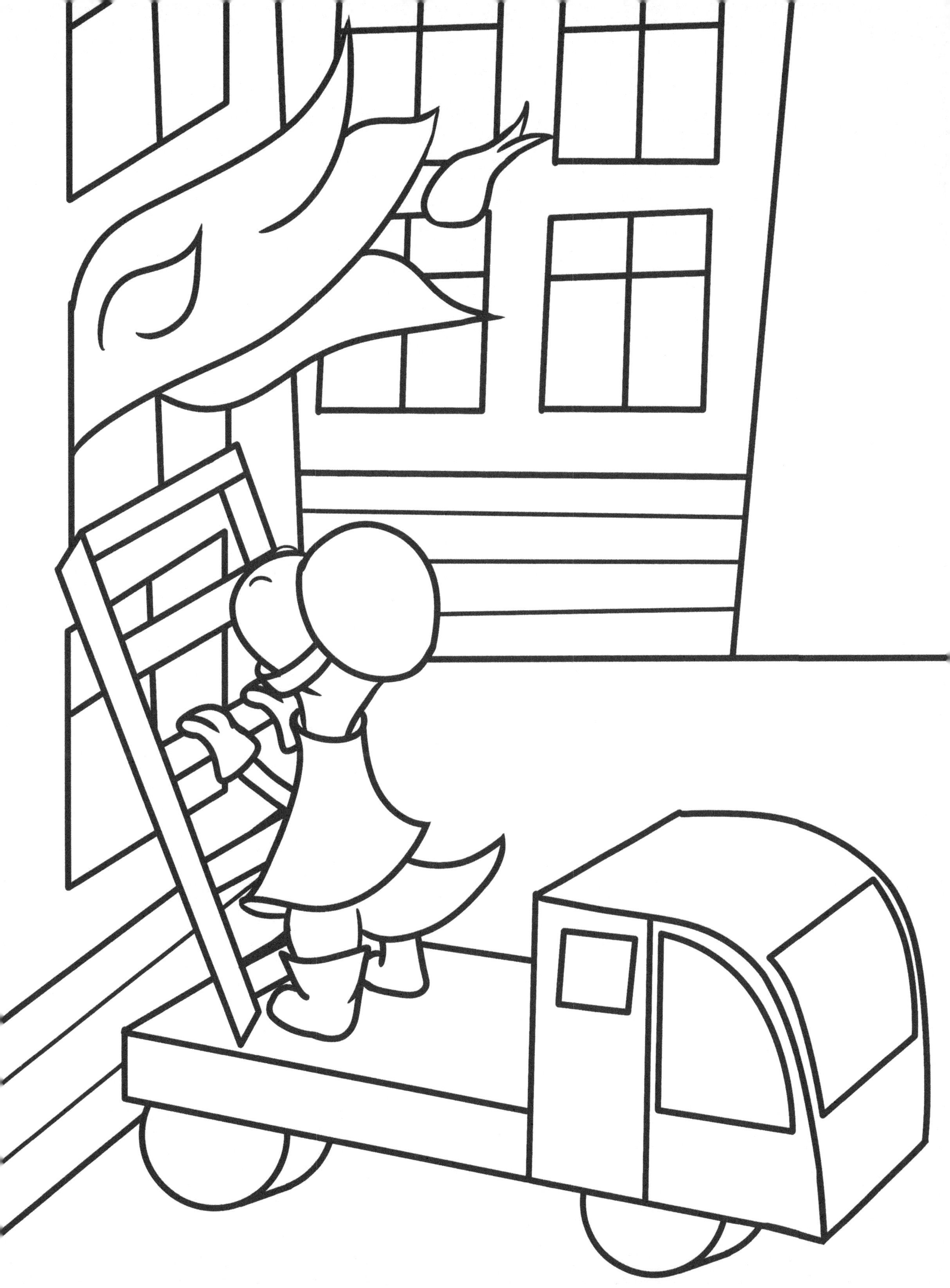

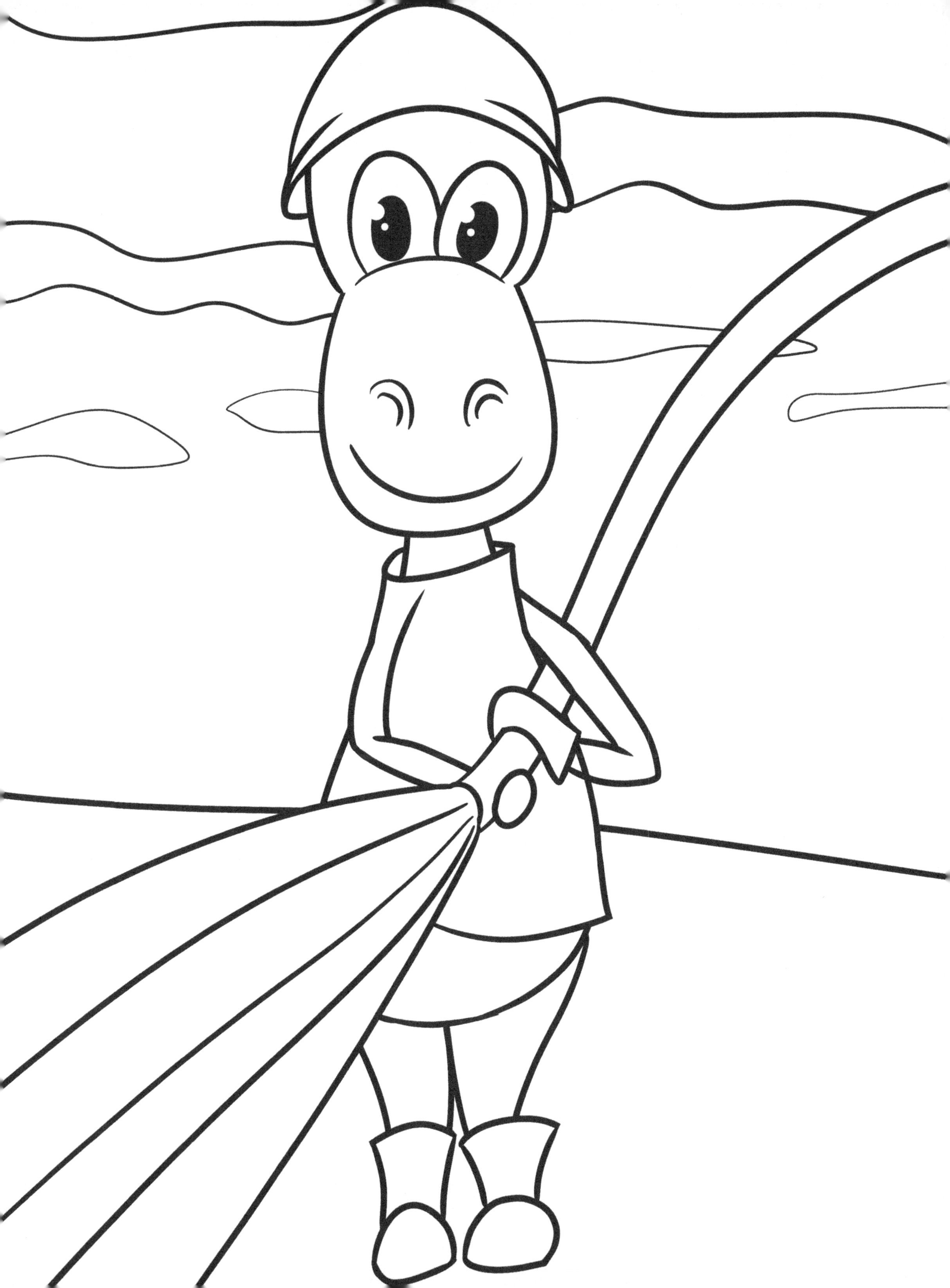

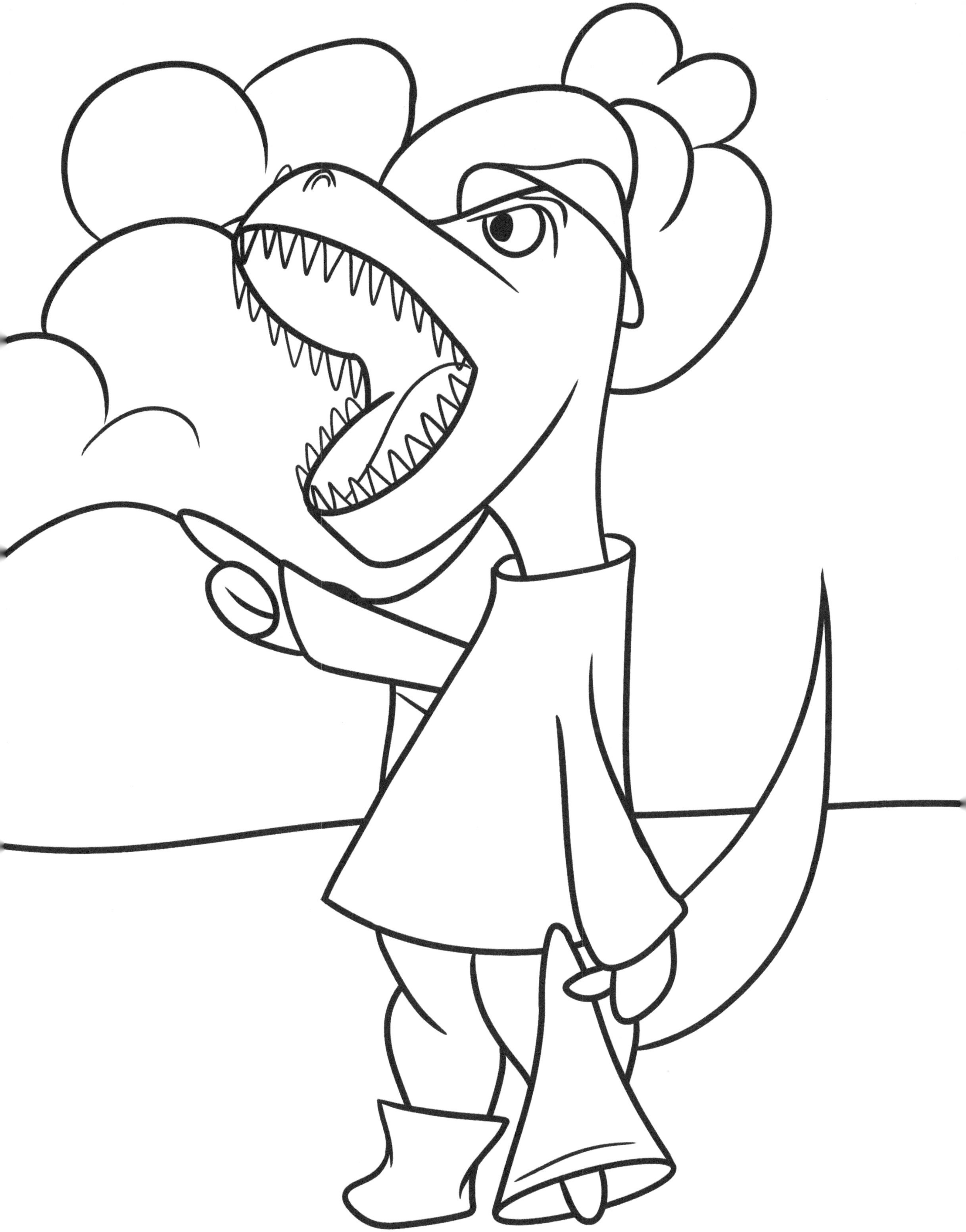

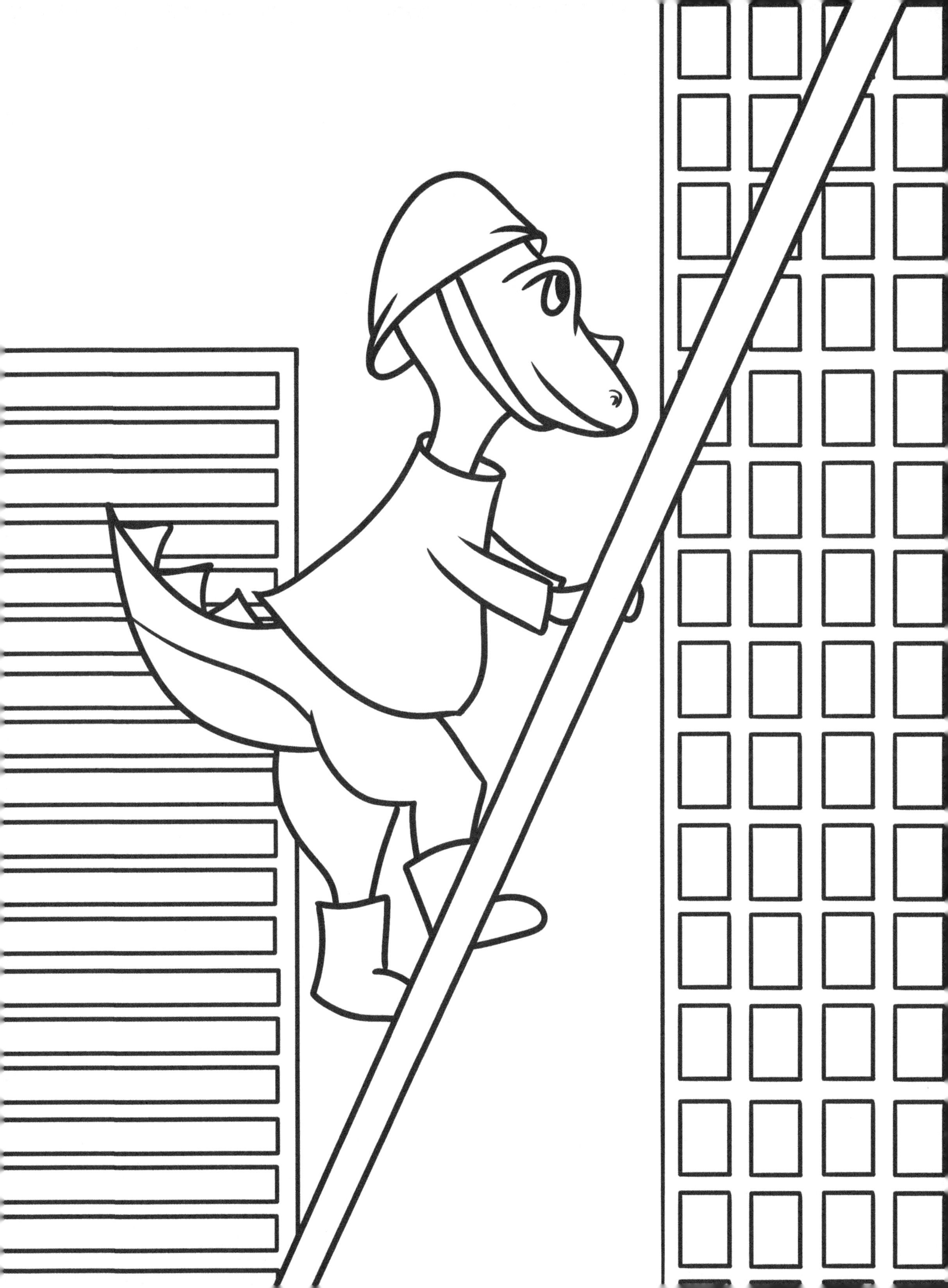

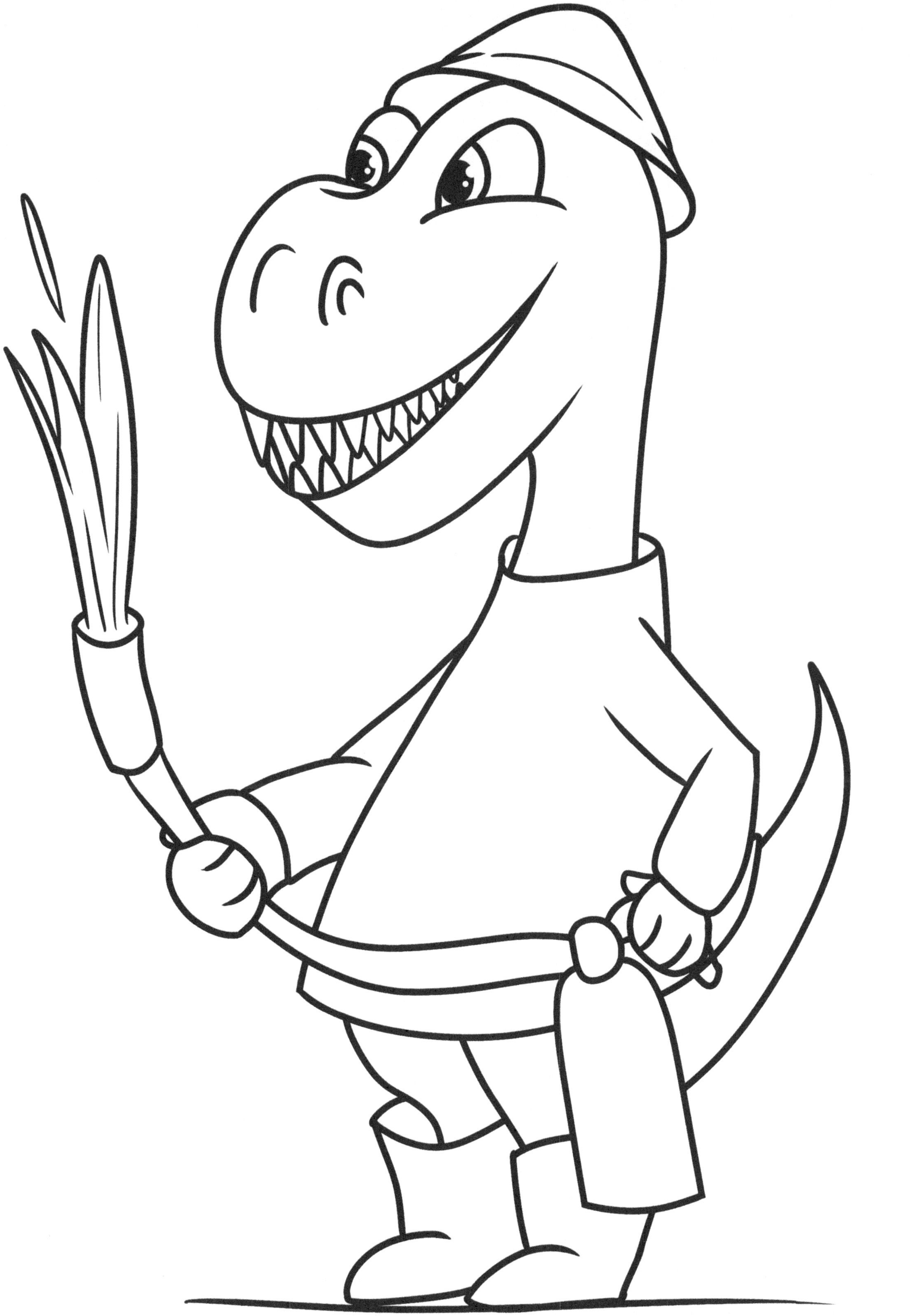

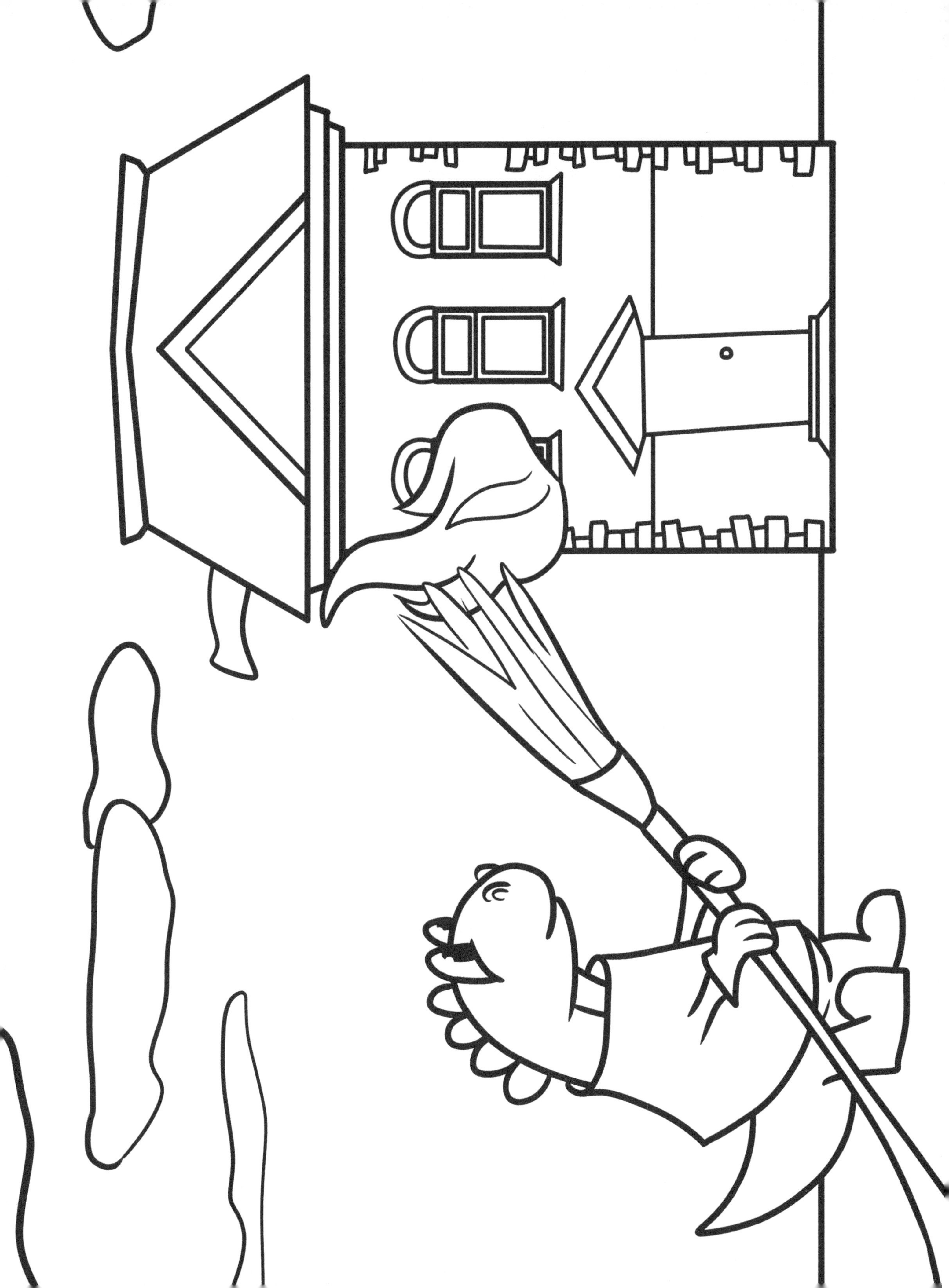

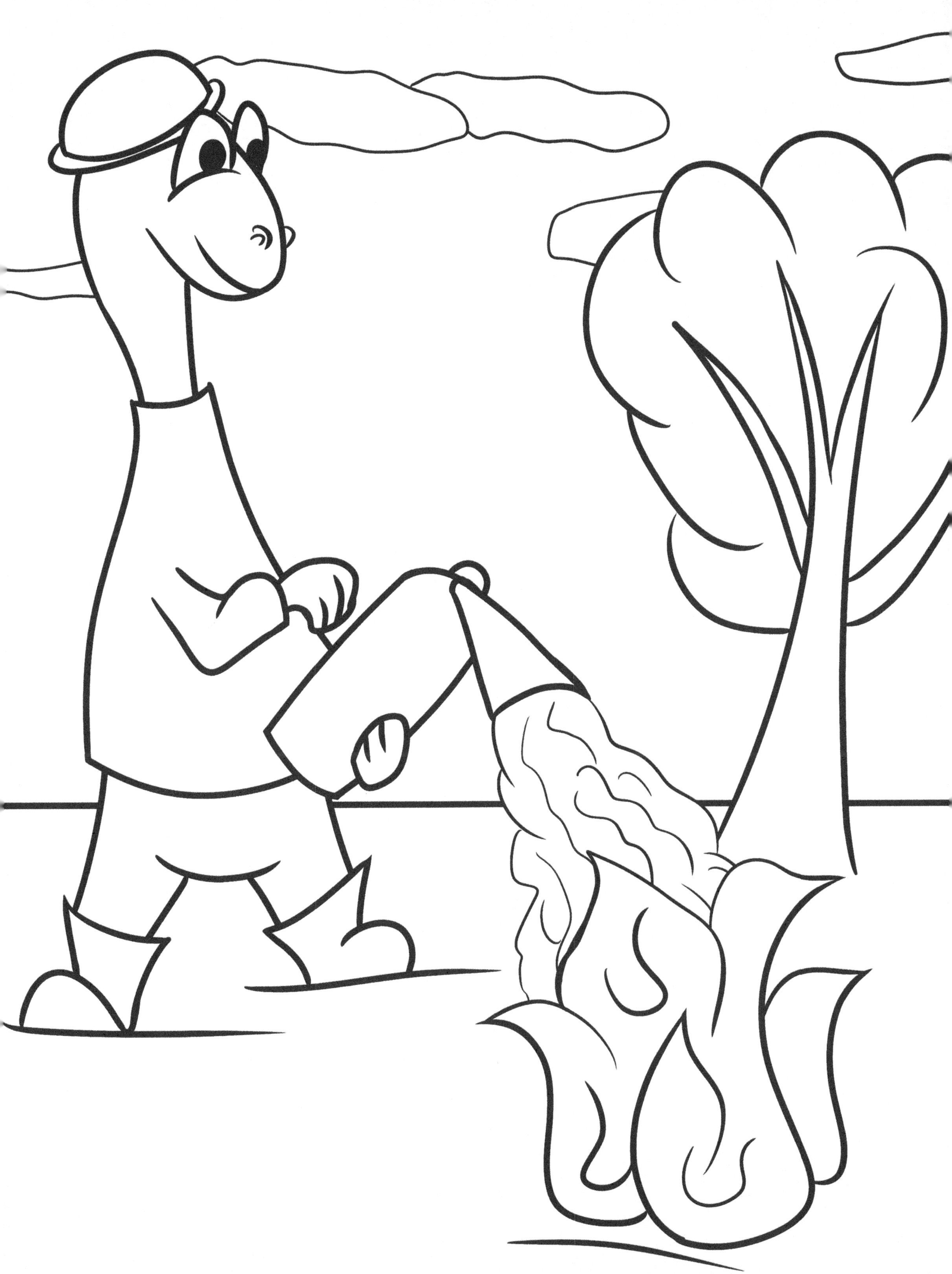

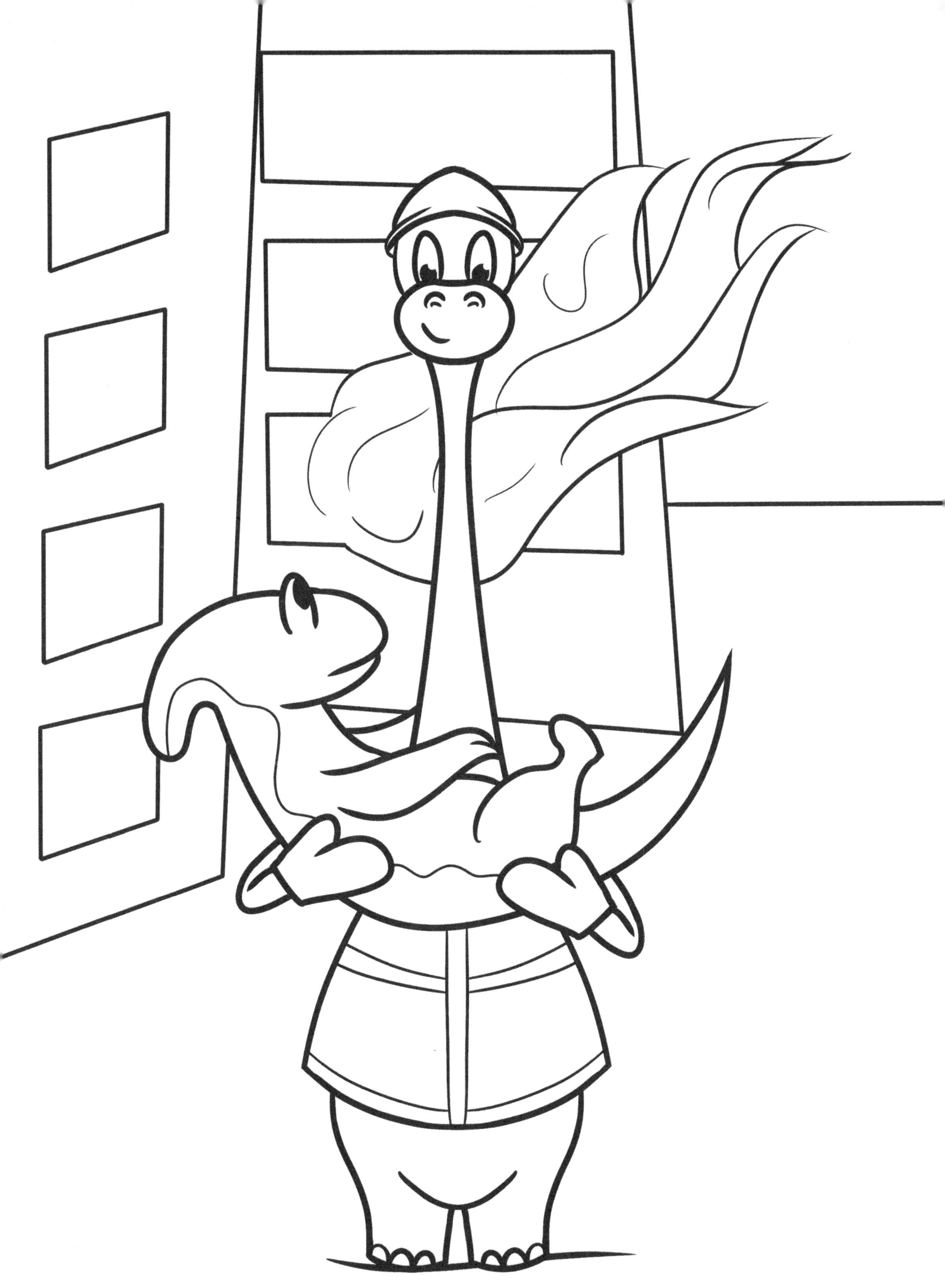

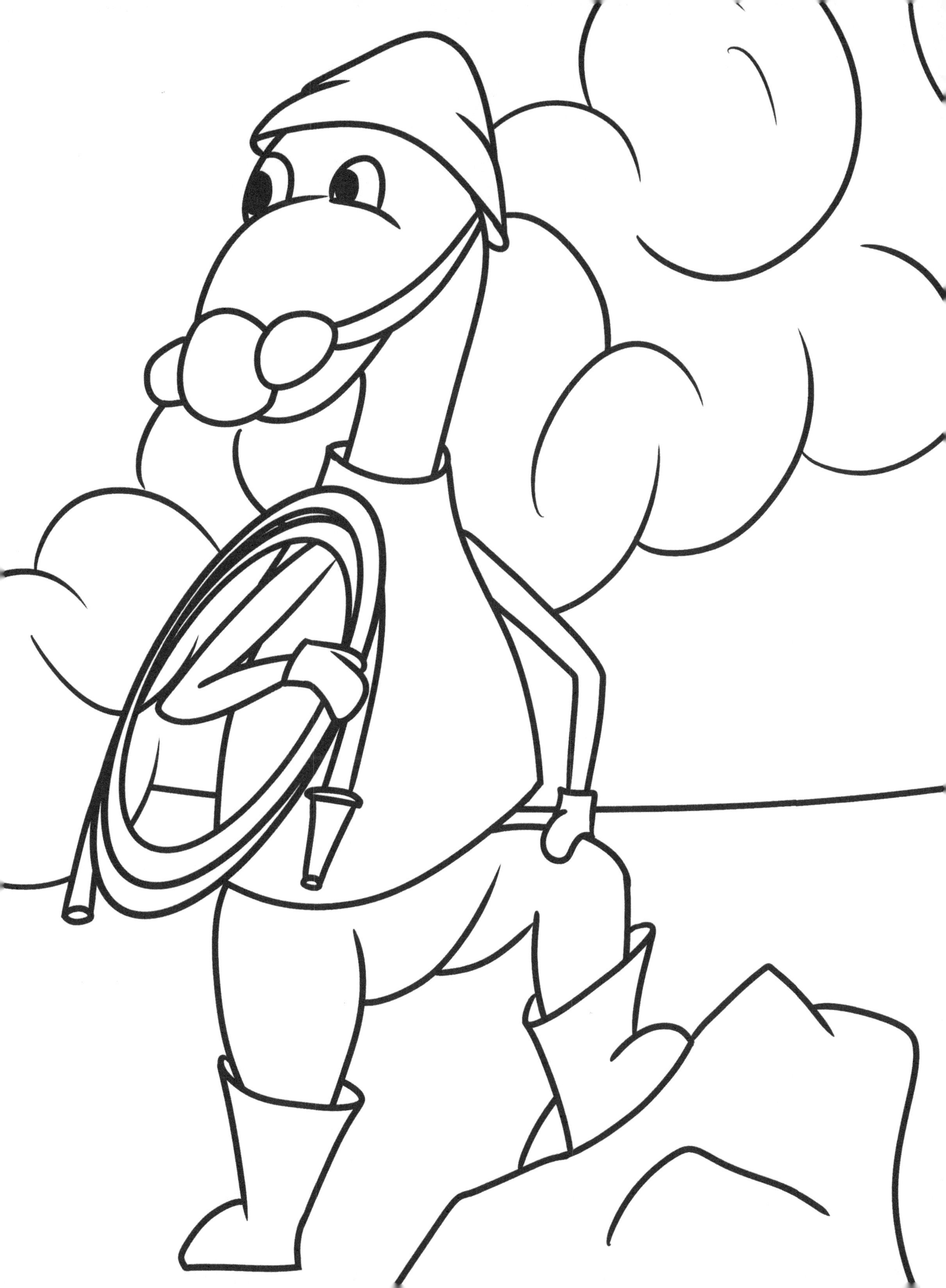

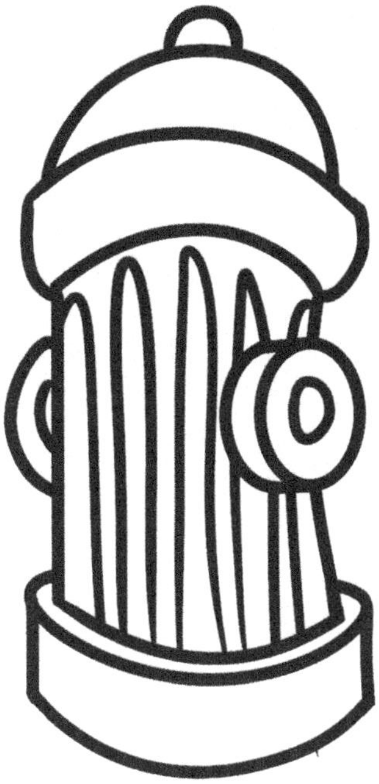
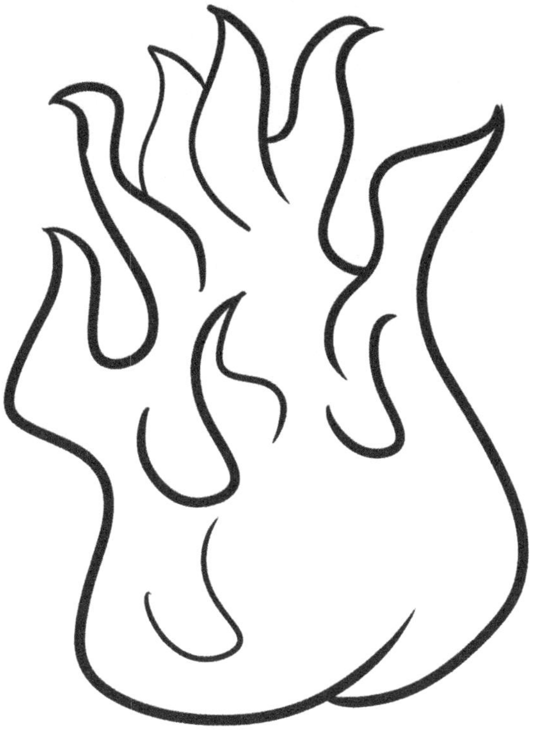
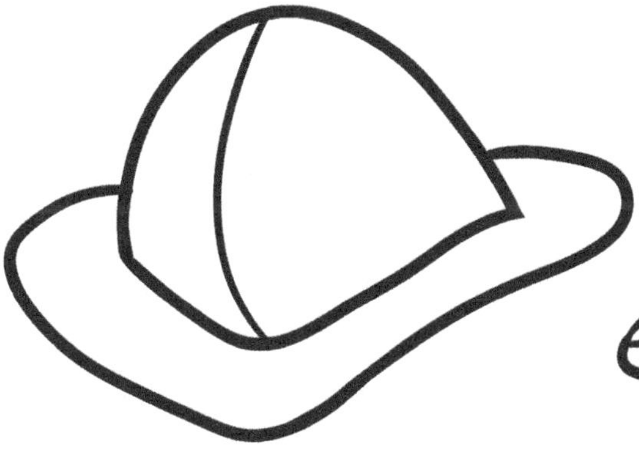
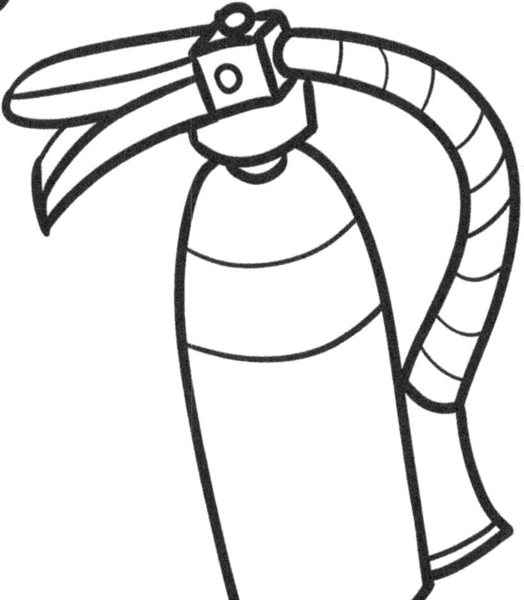
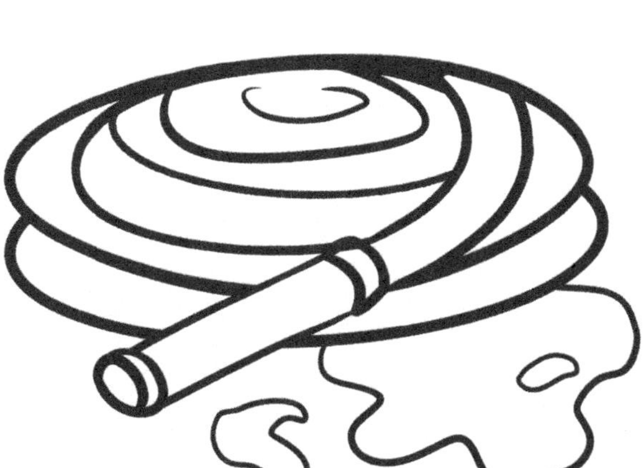

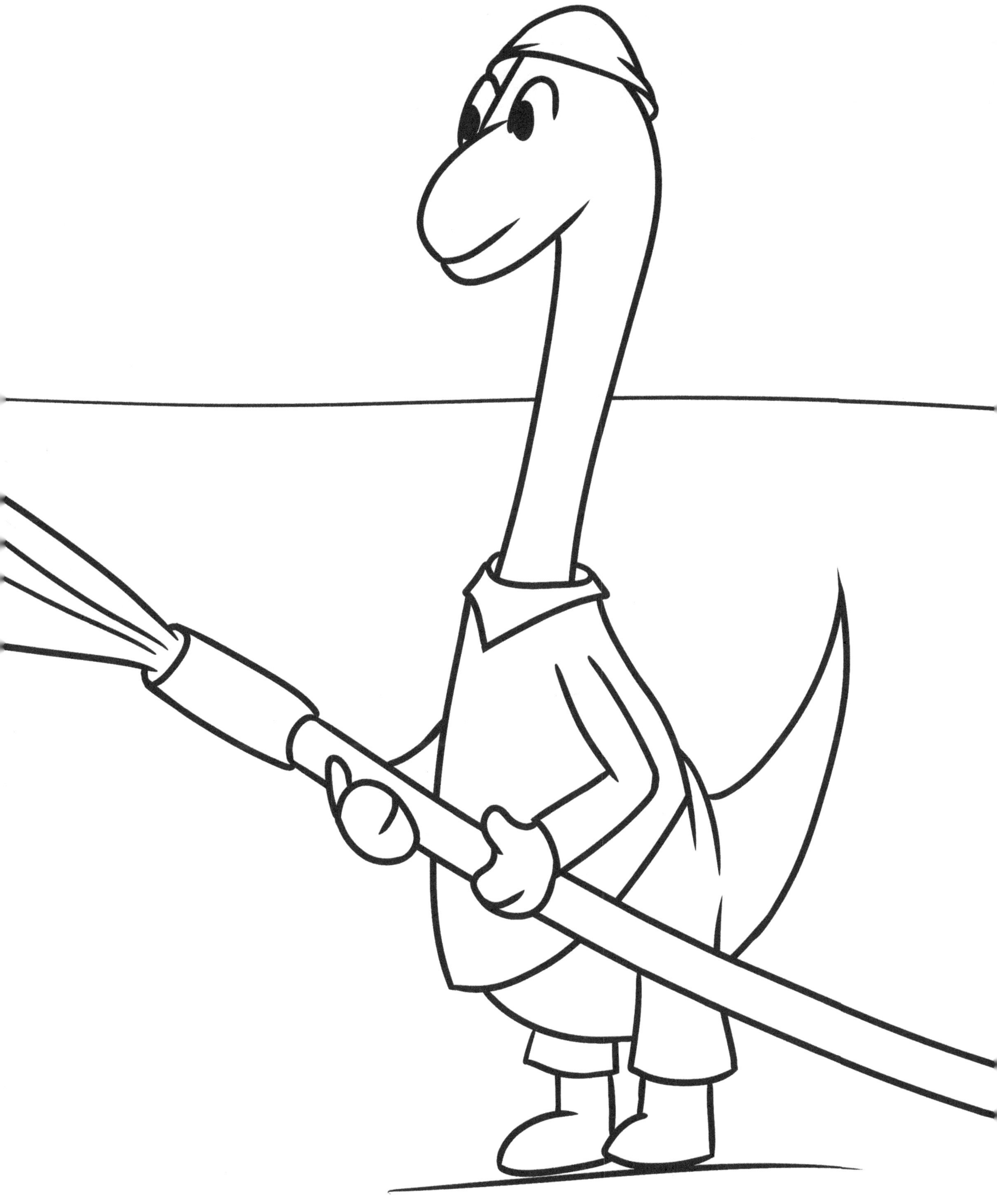

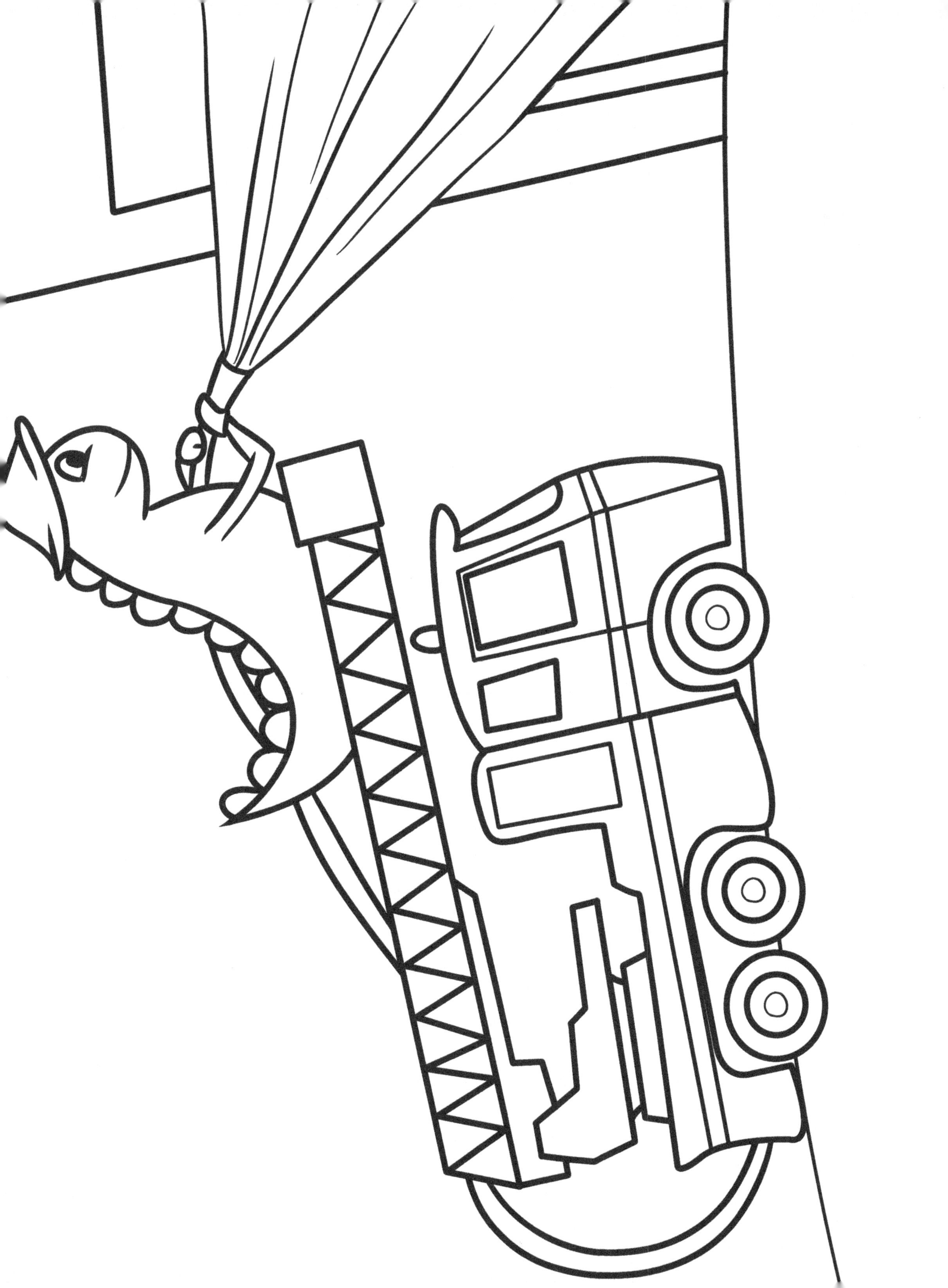

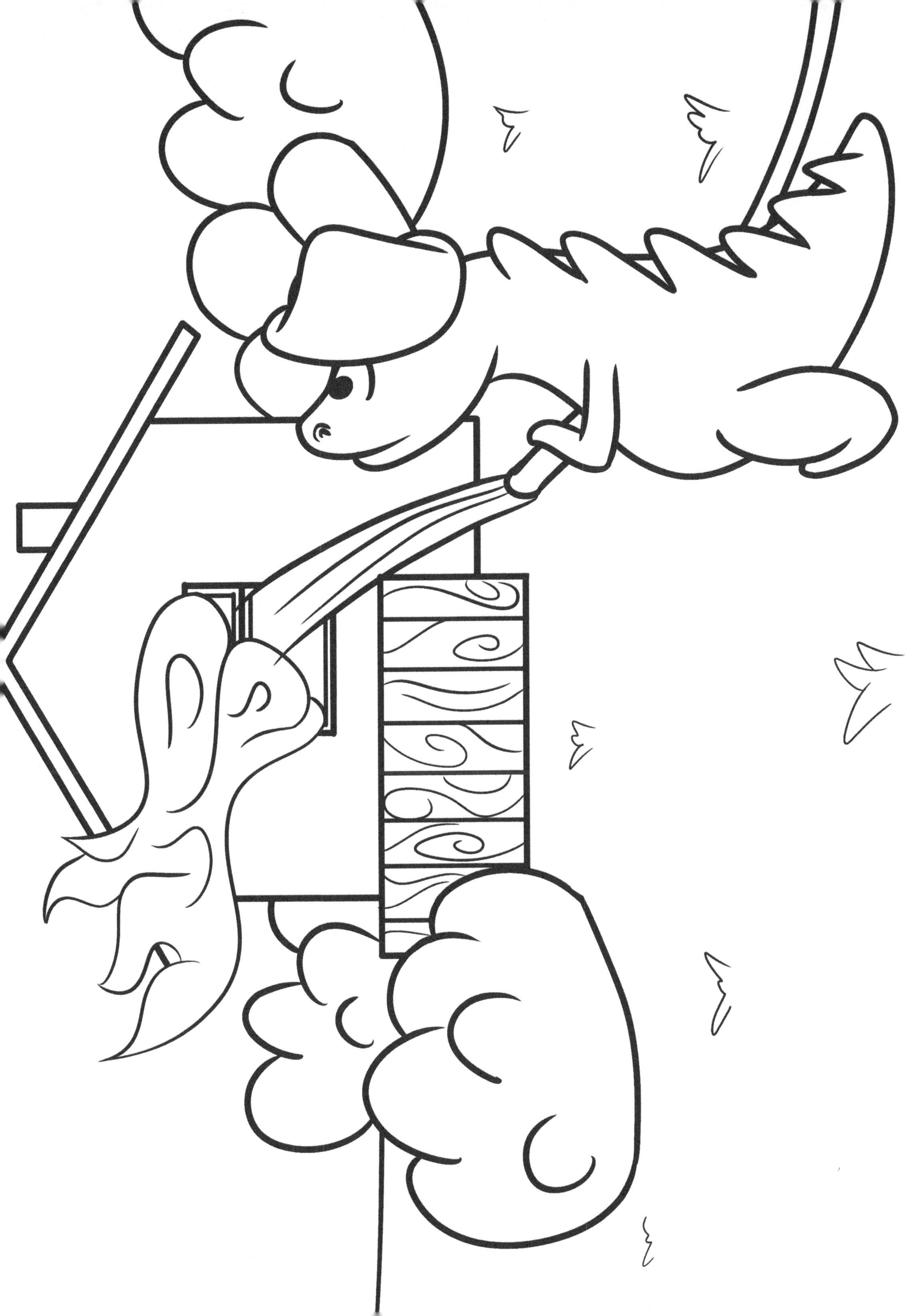

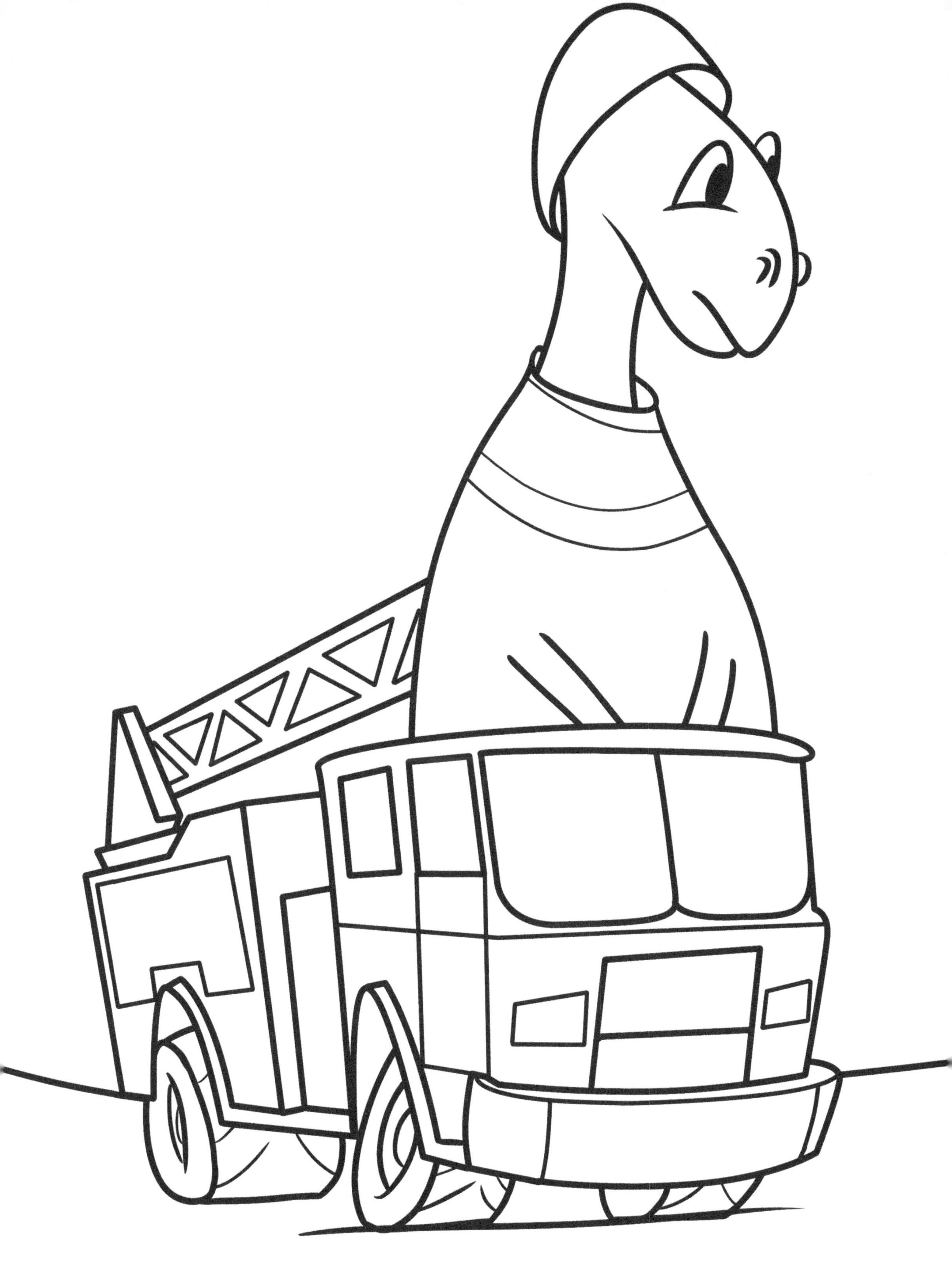

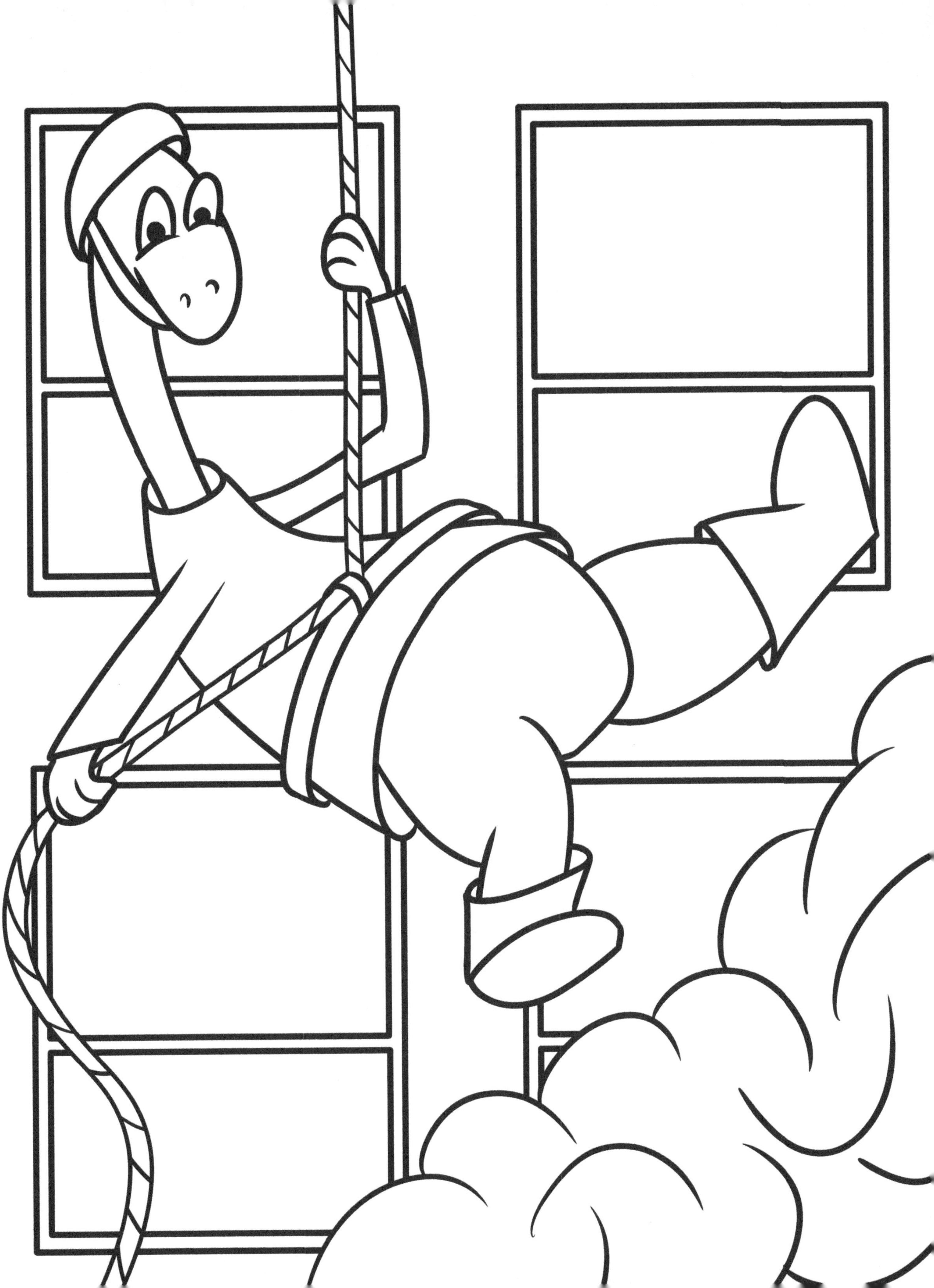

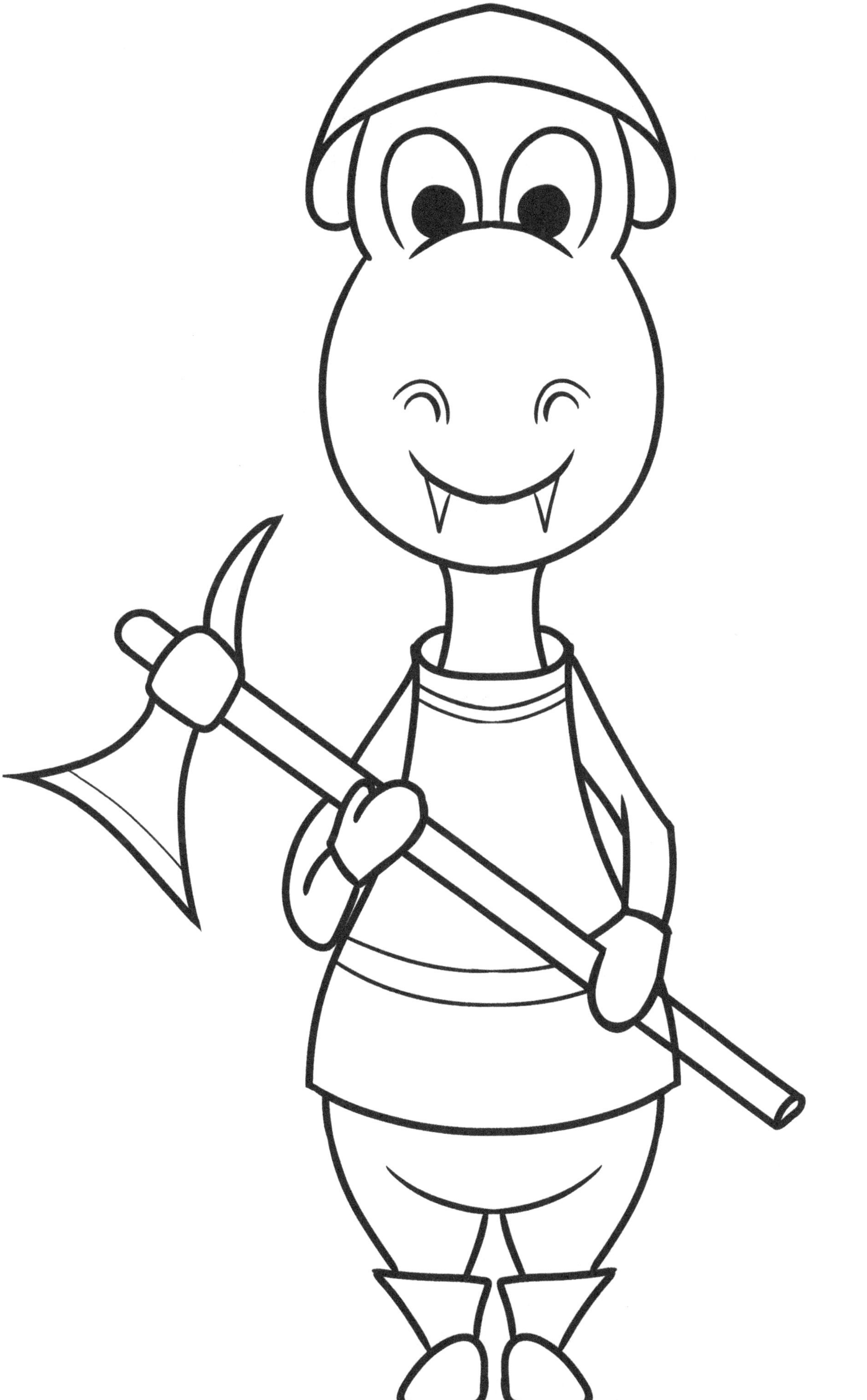

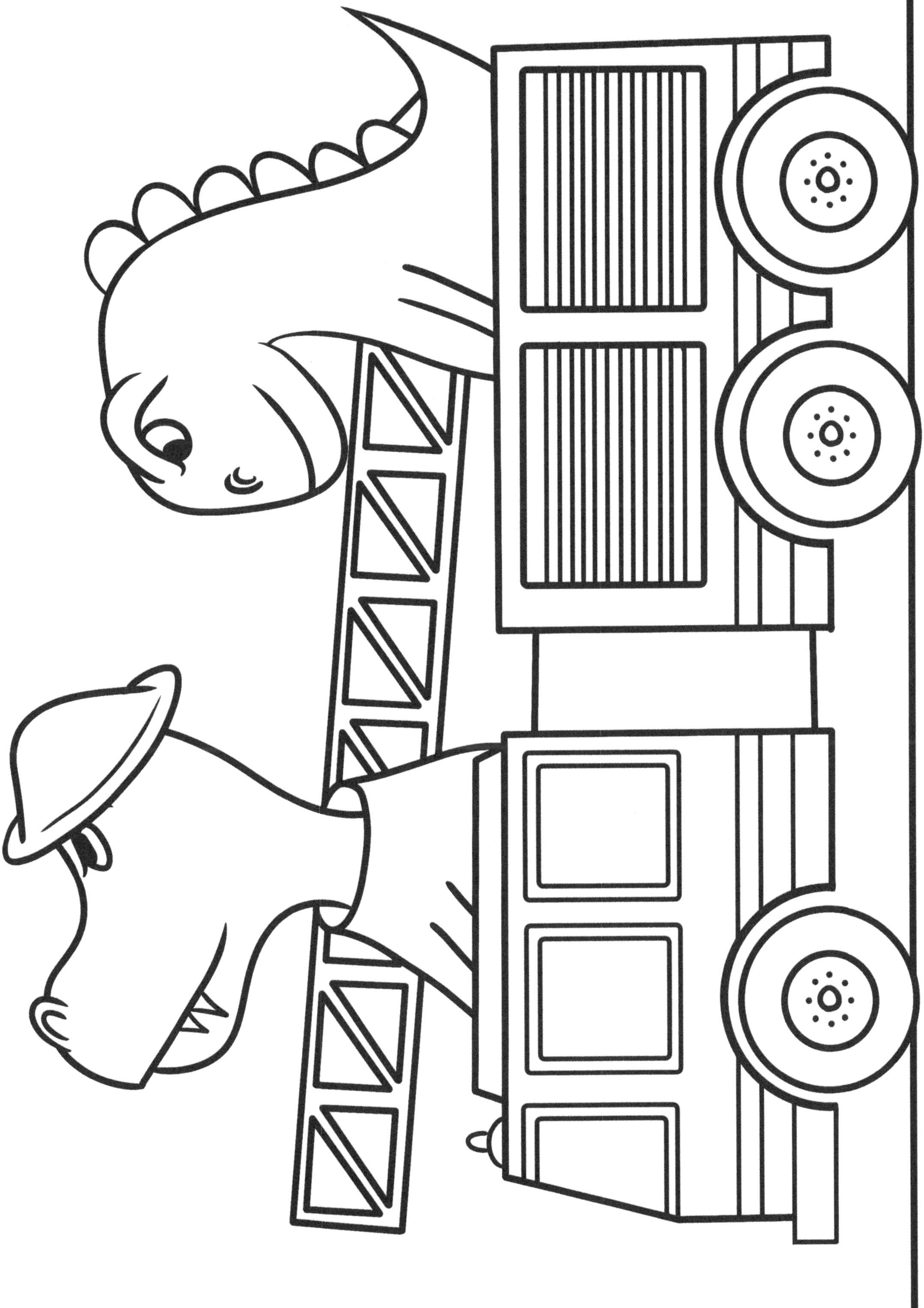

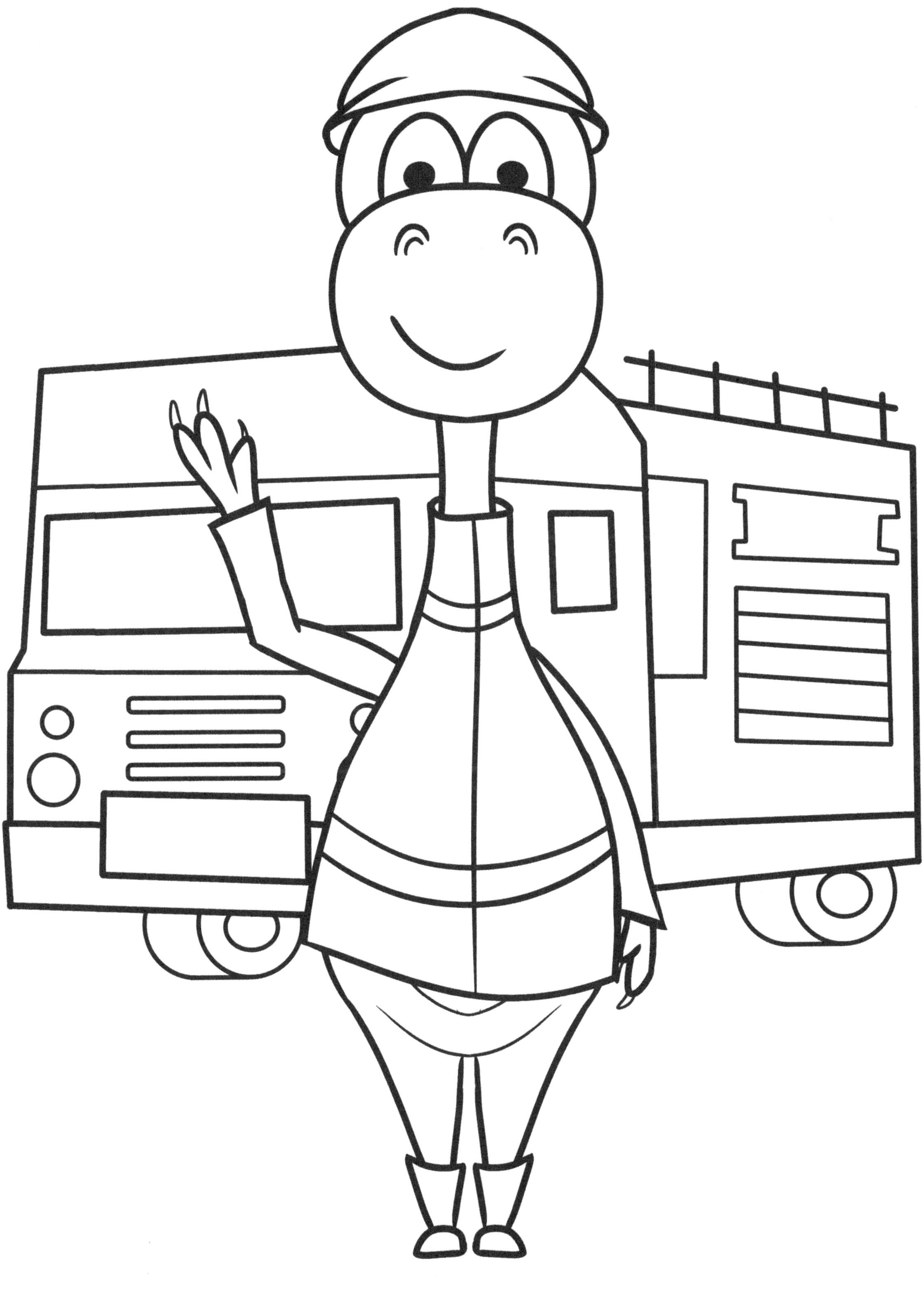

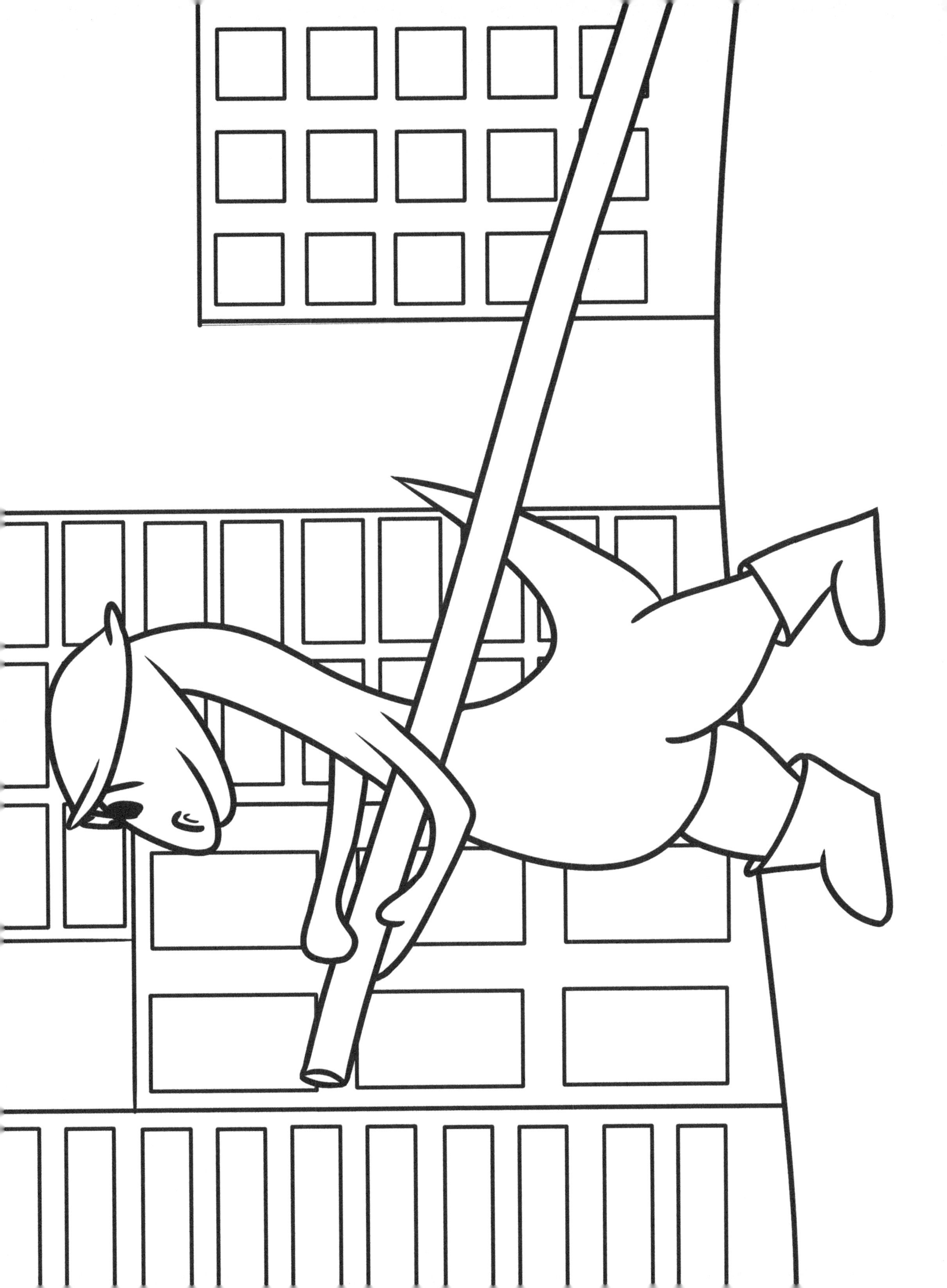

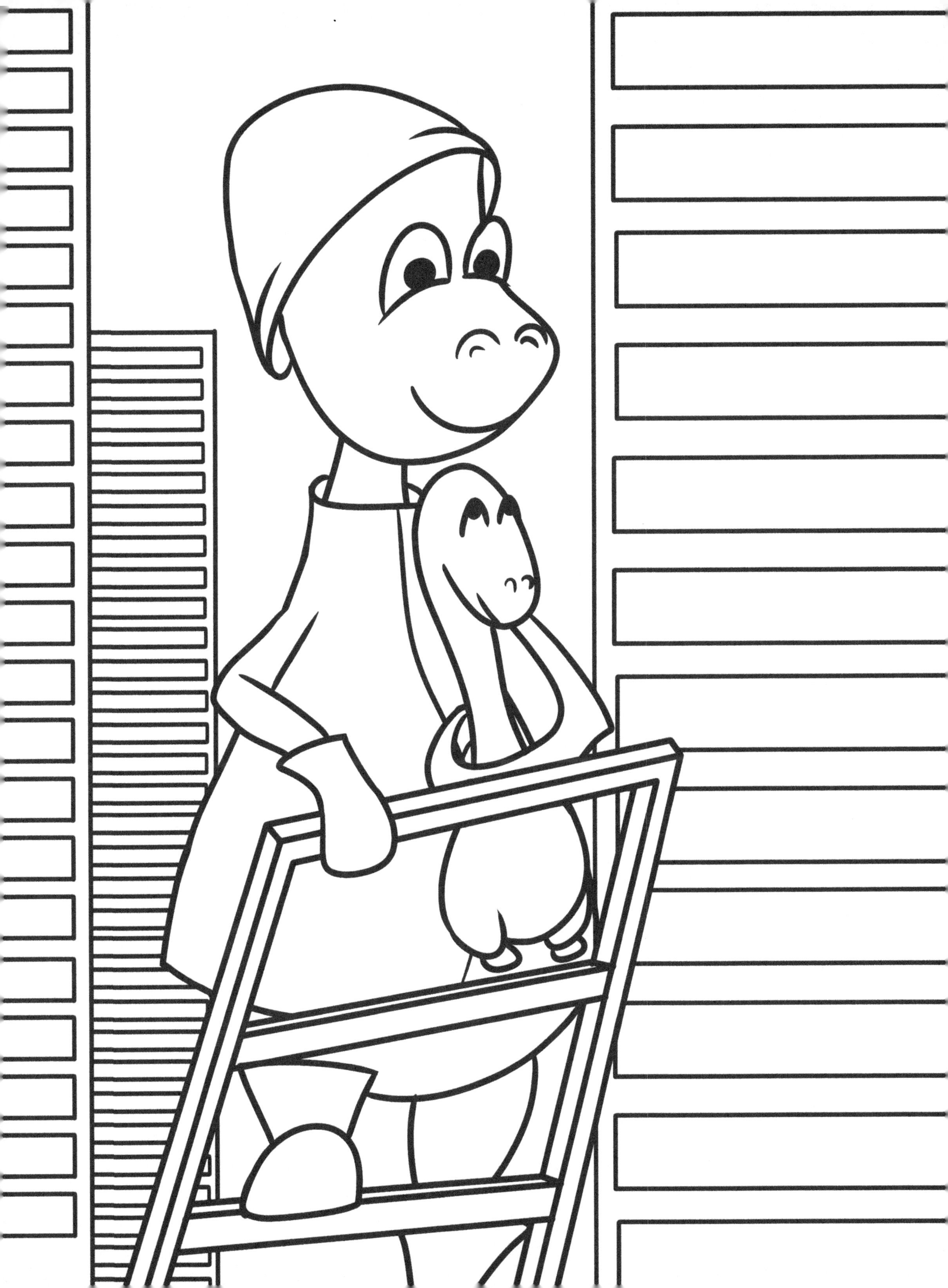

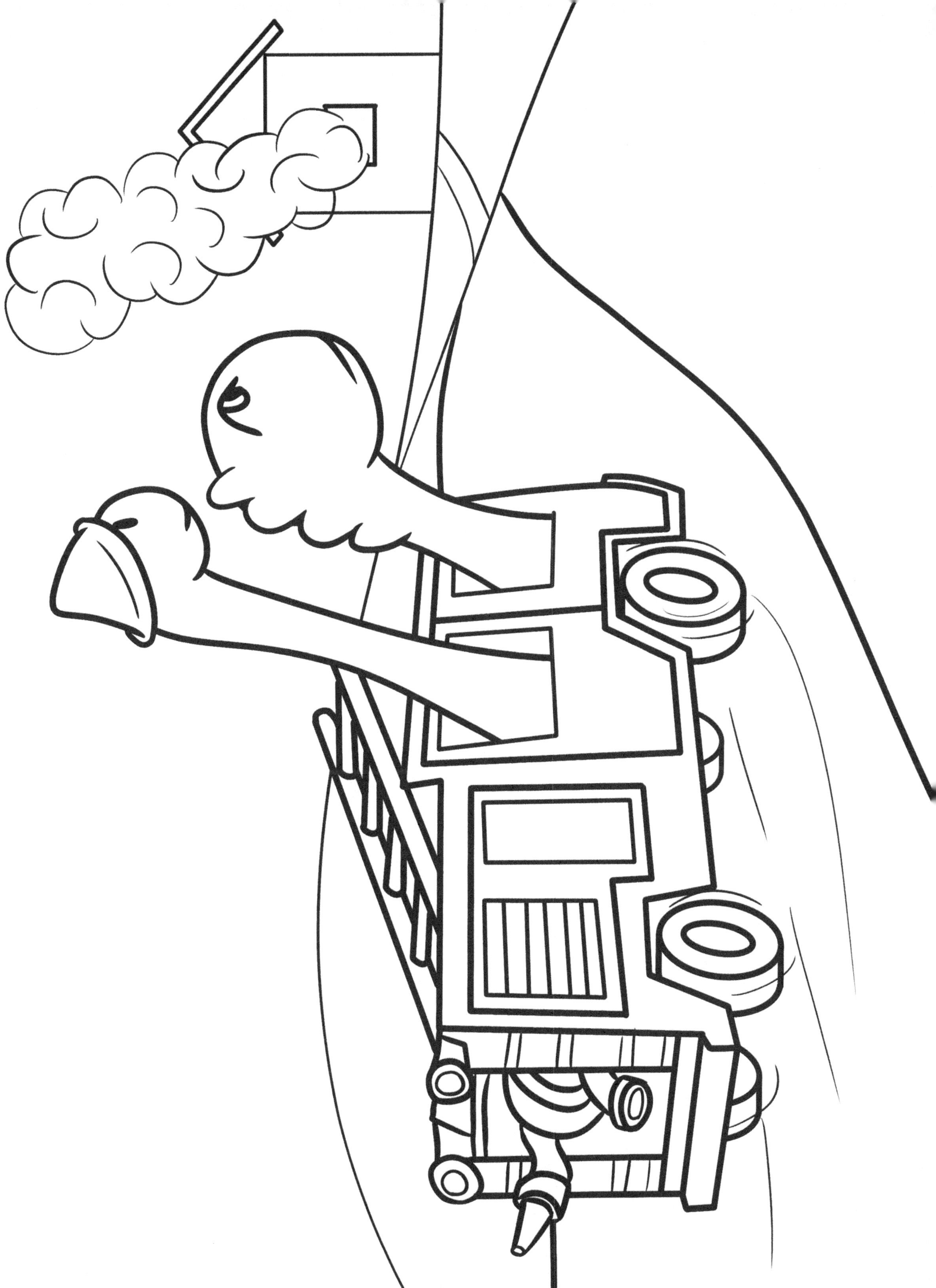

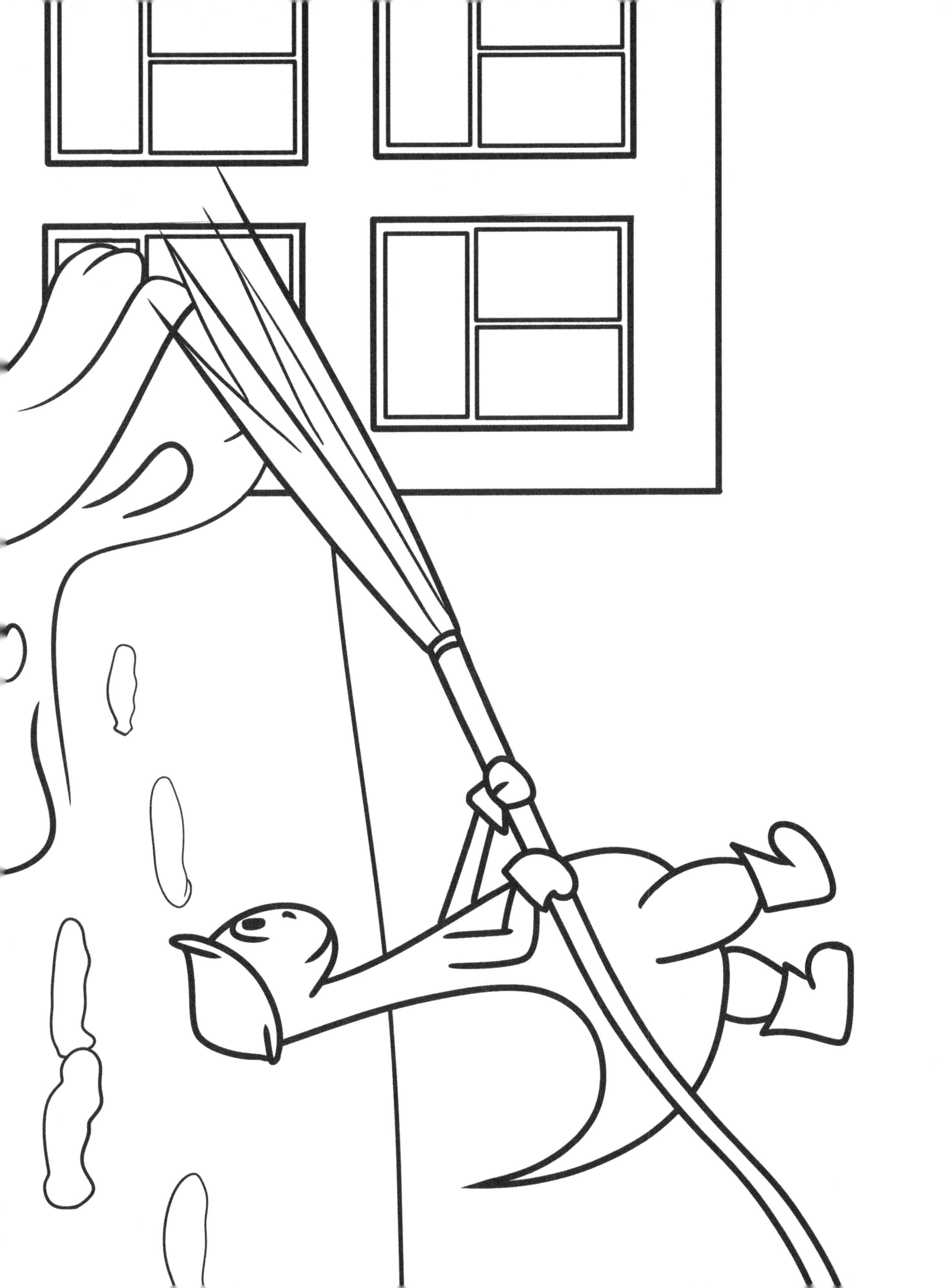

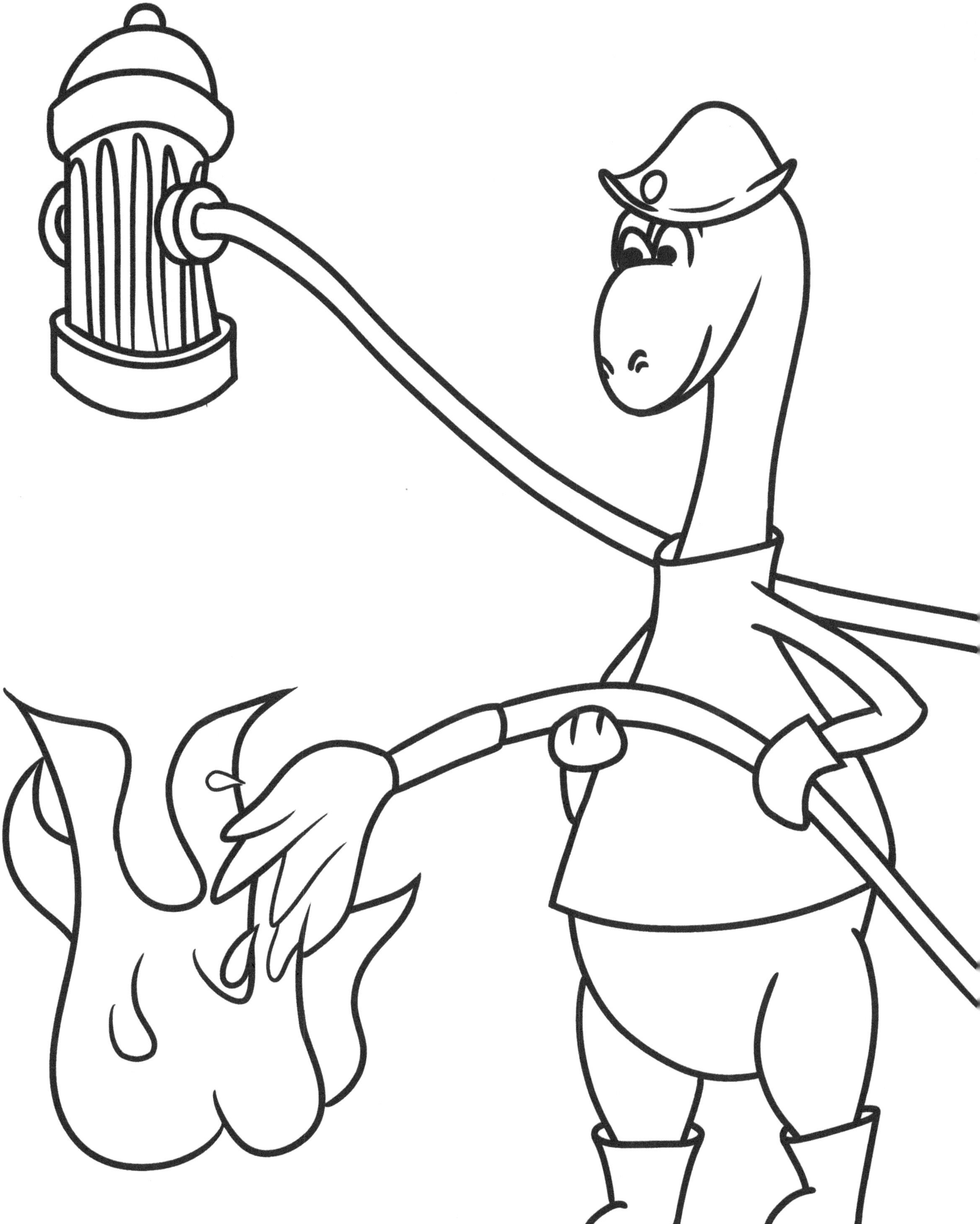

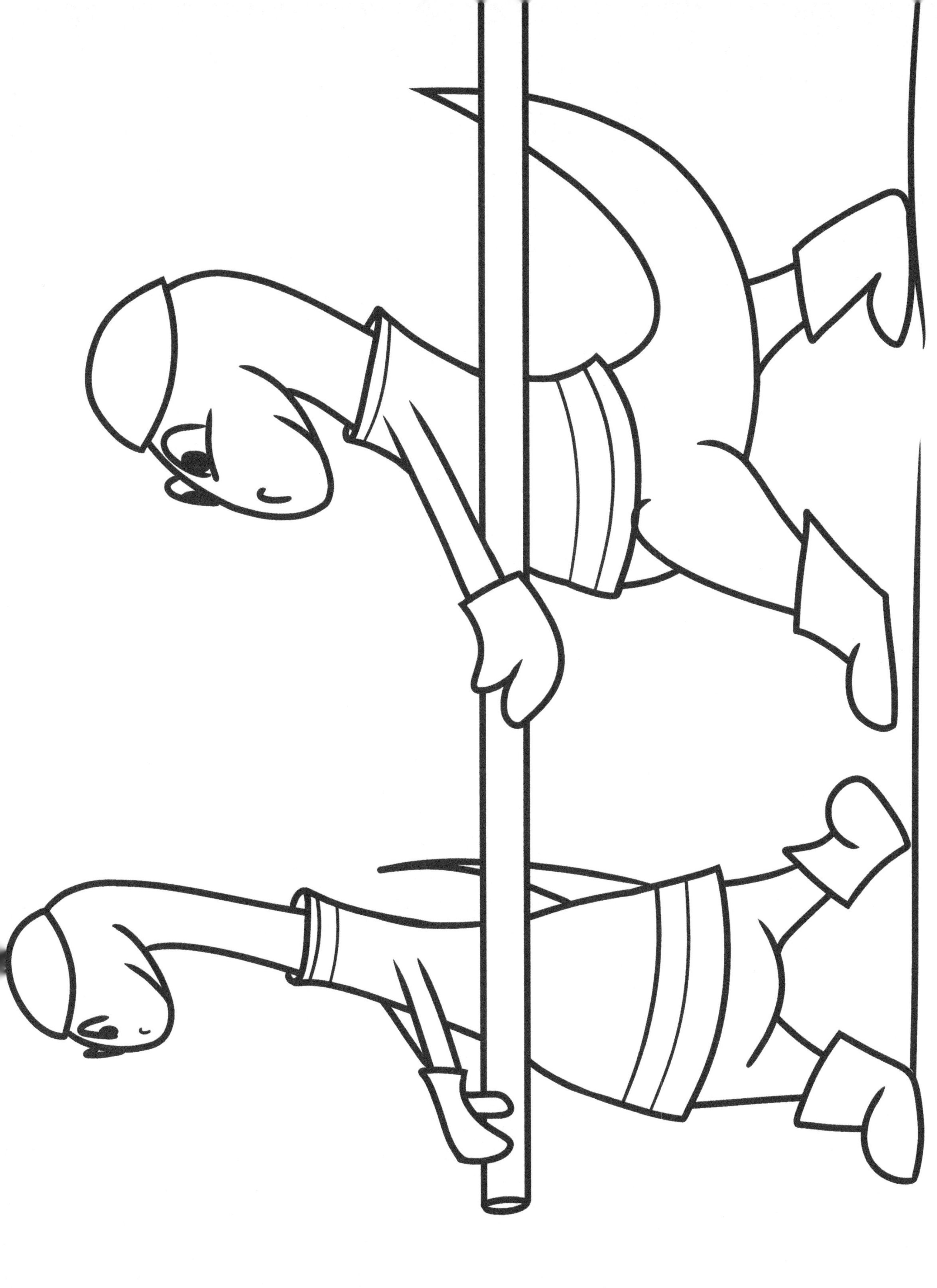

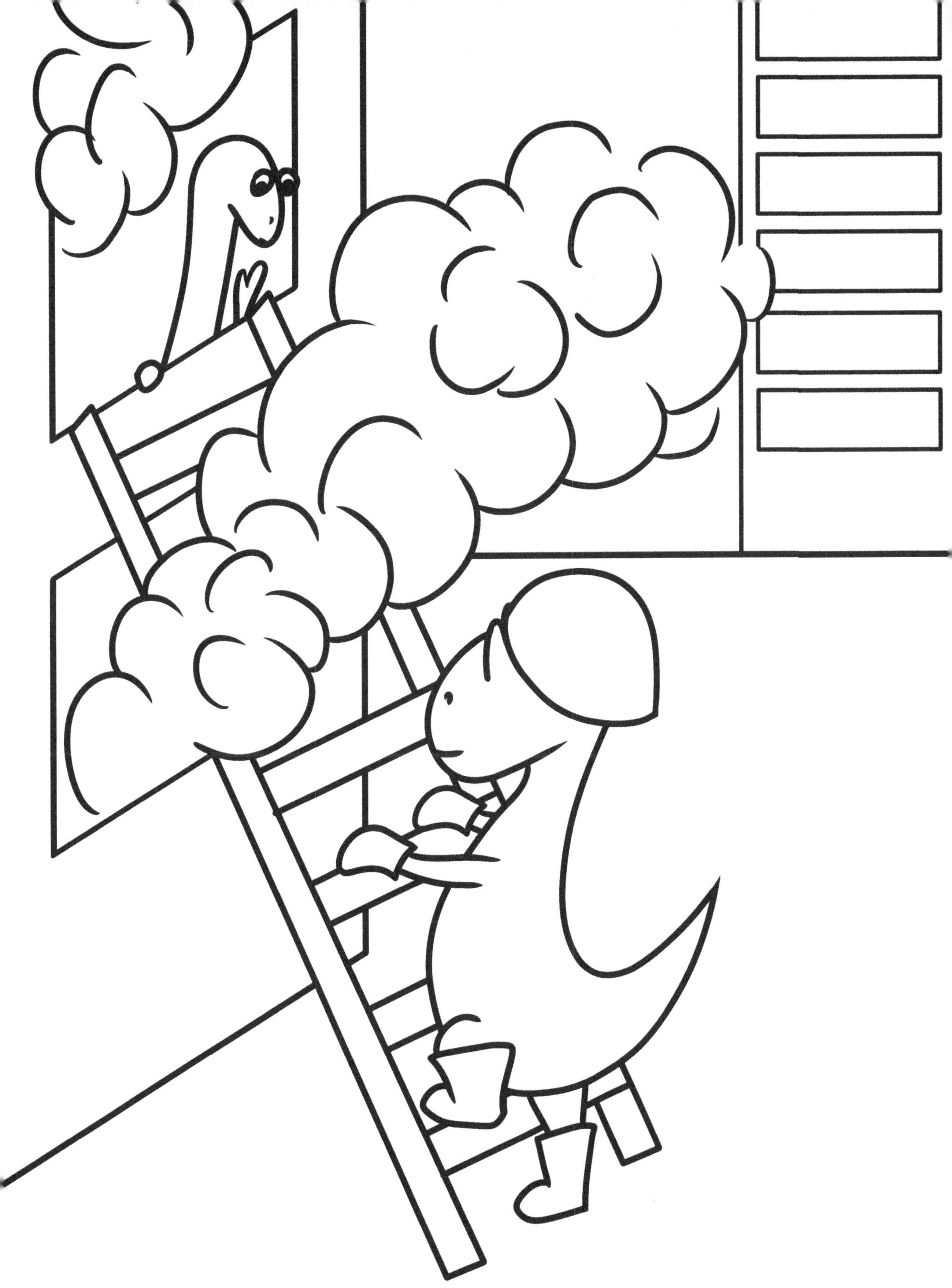

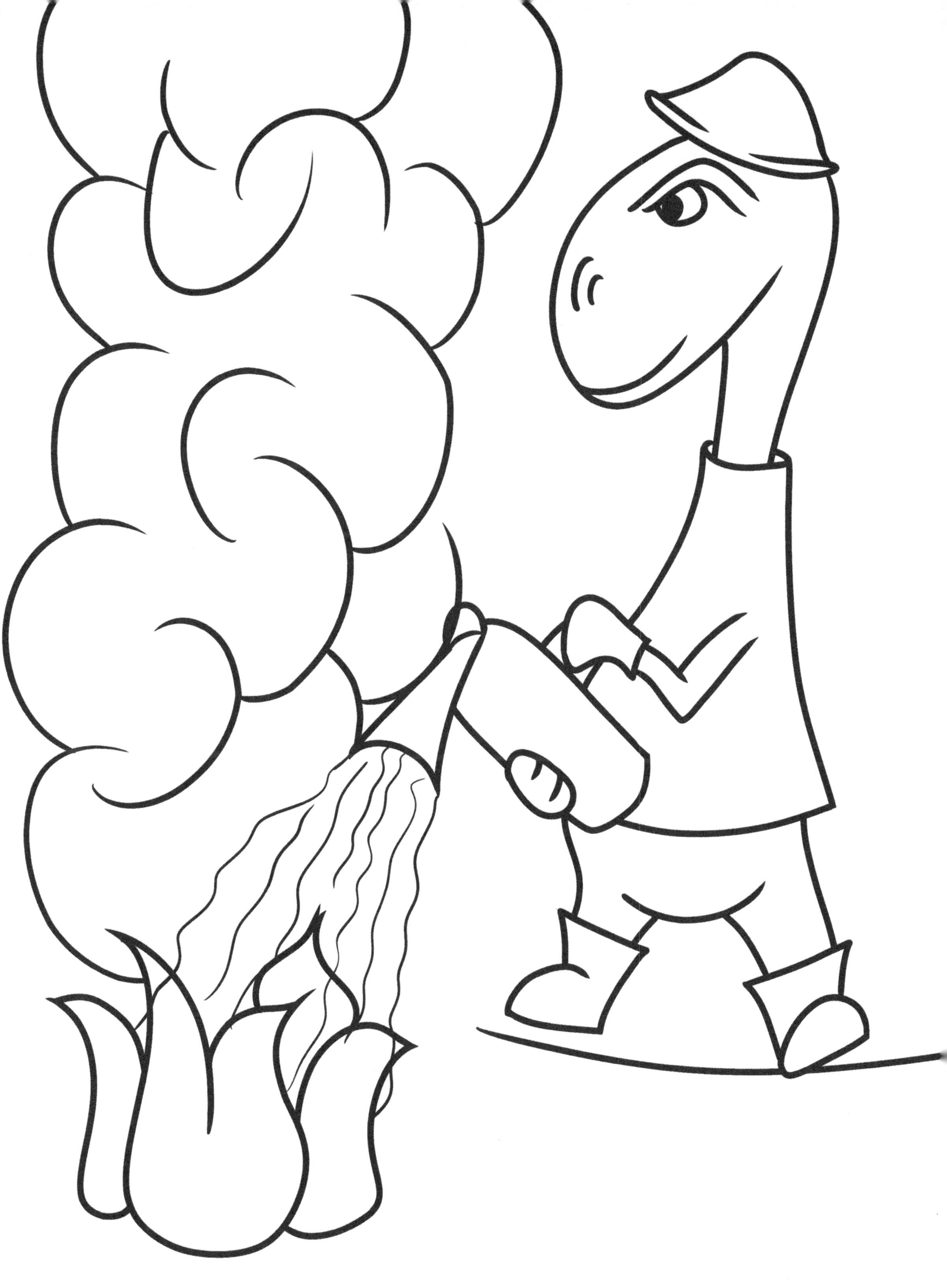

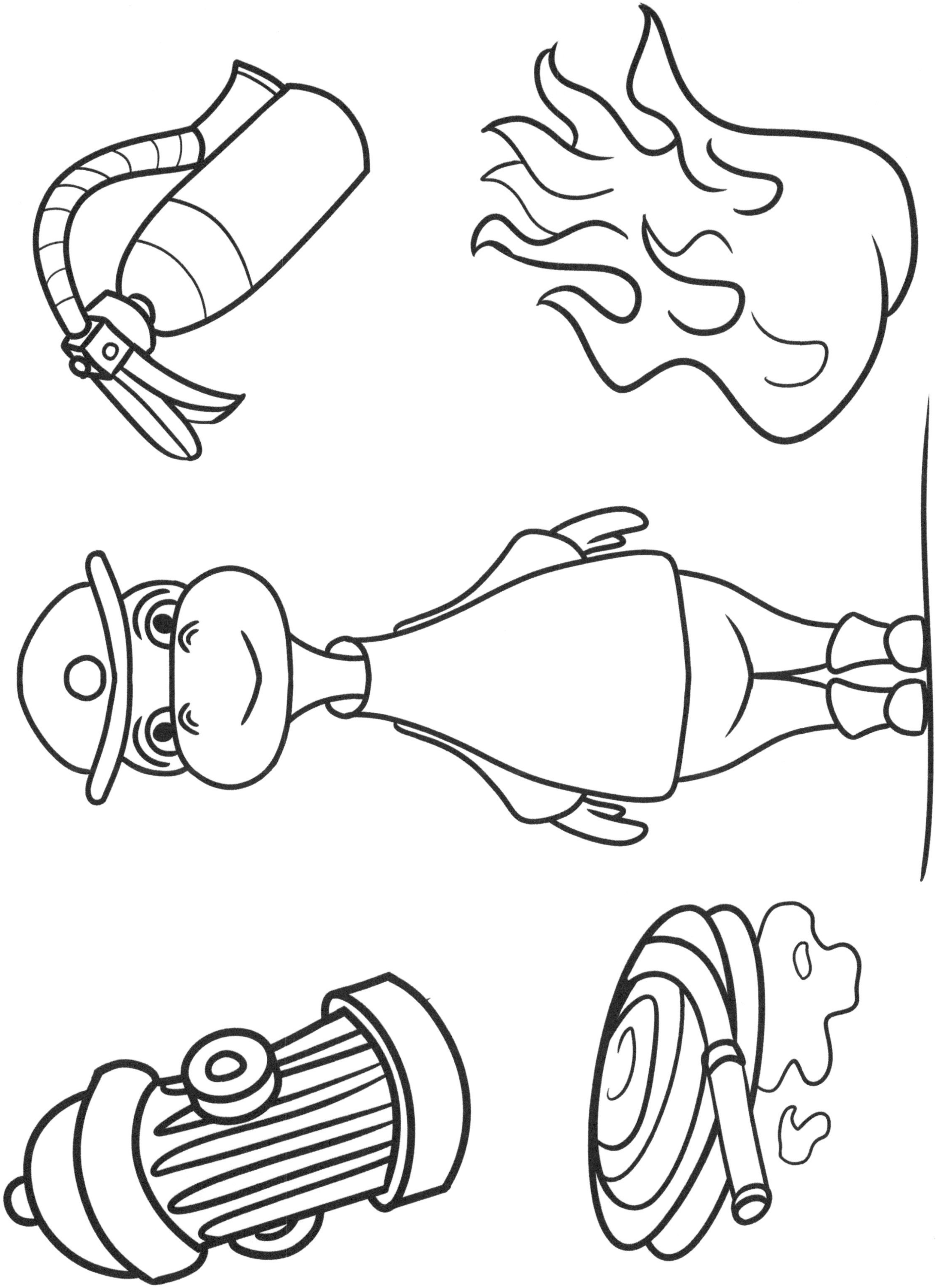